ENDORSEMENTS

The Identity Key is a hope-igniting book. Martina Davis brilliantly and effectively compares the destructive effects of five life-stealing mindset traps with the strengthening effects of five biblical principles of victory. She powerfully shares from her own experiences to illustrate and describe how she has worked through unhealthy mindsets with the Holy Spirit. She describes how a false identity weakens our core but that understanding our identity in Christ unlocks the fullness of our inheritance in God. I highly recommend this book.

— STEVE BACKLUND
Igniting Hope Ministries

I have known Martina and Richard since we attended the same church for many years. Martina and I were singers in the worship team, where we enjoyed wonderful moments of God's presence and worshipped with all of our being. Martina and Richard walked with me through ordination and encouraged me into my current role with the Armed Forces. Martina has taken up the challenge of this book with courage. She uses her experiences to effectively describe five mindset traps and replace them with biblical principles. I bless her book to be an inspiration and a guide to many on their spiritual journeys.

— PADRE JUSTIN BRADBURY

I have known Martina for just over twenty-five years, and in that time of our friendship she has grown in her spiritual life considerably. Martina has a wonderful way of using all her life experiences, good and bad, to bring glory to God; her relationship with Father God is so steadfast, sure, and incredibly intimate. I just love her writing and it keeps us all encouraged. One can only be strengthened in their faith by reading of such a great example.

— JANE COBURN

Lay Pastoral Assistant, All Saints, Swanage

I have been weaving elements of *The Posture Principle* into my daily life during lock-down and was eagerly anticipating the next instalment in the *Equipping Unexpected Warriors* series. *The Identity Key* does not disappoint. Martina's writing is vulnerable, refreshing, authentic, alive, relatable, hope-giving and clearly rooted in a deep love of Jesus and close friendship with our Father. These transformative books have been written for such a time as this. There is so much more!

— TESS EVANS

Founder of InfoSec Matters and EveryDayBest

It has been a joy to watch Martina working on this book. I have been with her on this journey over the last thirty-eight years although, as I guess is the case in many marriages, I had not been completely aware of all her thinking!

Our journey together has been a delight. As you will read, we have had to overcome many challenges. With young children, busy jobs and more recently with advent of the 'always-available' culture, it has been full on. But what I have seen throughout is the amount of time she has devoted, and continues to devote, to making the space to have time with God, and the fruit which this has brought.

Sometimes faith is a struggle. A struggle with your inner thoughts, a struggle with your environment or just simply a struggle to find the time. Although it can be hard, it often helps to step back and invest the time to work out exactly what is going on. Martina has, I now realise, done this often over the years.

When stripped down, the underlying issues which prevent our realising our true identity in Christ, although well camouflaged, can be surprisingly simple. In this book she offers a distillation of the common obstacles on the route to a deeper faith and practical ways to think and pray about them, and thus find solutions.

— RICHARD DAVIS

the
IDENTITY
KEY

the
IDENTITY
KEY

MARTINA DAVIS

 Zaccmedia

Published by Zaccmedia
www.zaccmedia.com
info@zaccmedia.com

Published November 2020

ISBN: 978-1-911211-99-0

British Library Cataloguing-in-Publication Data
A catalogue record for this book is available from the British Library.

Zaccmedia aims to produce books that will help to extend and build up the Kingdom of God. We do not necessarily agree with every view expressed by the authors, or with every interpretation of Scripture expressed. We expect readers to make their own judgment in the light of their understanding of God's Word and in an attitude of Christian love and fellowship.

_____

Unexpected Warriors are those who
  thought they had no voice.

God gives us a voice to declare freedom.

He lights a fire of hope within us.

Throughout those places where the flame
  of hope is taken,

Bones will be shaken, not with terror, but
  by laughter.

As they are shaken, the flesh will build on
  them and the muscle and sinew,

And they will find new talents and skills,

Because their fingers are working, and
  their feet will walk.

These are the sons and daughters of God.

Their hearts will be lifted

And they will be proclaimers of the deeds
  of God

And the presence of God.

— MARTINA

CONTENTS

ACKNOWLEDGEMENTS

I would not have accomplished this book without the willing, sacrificial, and talented help of several people.

Richard, my husband, you have been a motivator, experienced coach and a prayerful, challenging companion both during the writing and editing of this book, and in the coming into being of long-held dreams and desires. Sensitively drawing me out on certain topics, you have made the manuscript so much richer by encouraging me to think more deeply and express myself. I could not walk this journey without you. We are blessed to be so different, expressly so that we can help one another in our blind spots. You've always believed in me, and drawn me out to be so much more.

James and David, our sons, thank you for being who you are. You are both great, inspirational encouragers and true adventurers, full of insights and down-to-earth wisdom.

Jane Coburn, you have been such a faithful friend for over twenty-five years. We have walked through much. Thank you for your truthful comments and many reads of the manuscript, prayerful encouragement, and endorsement of my work and life.

Mark Iles, my mentor and encourager for the past seven years, thank you for your prophetic insights, truth-speaking and challenge that have helped me to walk this path. Thank you for travelling faithfully with me and committing to me your experience and wisdom to carry forward and break into the new. I have learned so much from you.

Steve Backlund and the Igniting Hope Team! You have consistently released joy, encouragement and insight to me. Thank you for reviewing and endorsing my book and my life. As a part of that wonderful gift of hope that you carry, you have continued to thoughtfully empower me, and make me laugh!

Tess Evans, what a sparky, life-filled friend and help on this journey you have been! Thank you for your reading, edits and suggestions with prayer, with endorsement of my life and writing.

My friends who have prayed for me and my writing, been 'book midwives' along the way, and our church family at Winchester Vineyard – thank you. Many of you have inspired my journey, by your journeys.

Paul Stanier at Zaccmedia, you are always a great help to me, with your organisational skills and encouraging attitude. Thank you!

FOREWORD

BY MARK ILES

While I described Martina's previous book as an inspirational guidebook on intimacy, this book on the other hand is a major proclamation of the gospel and has serious 'teeth'. It could be described as a practical answer to the five horsemen of the sub-normal Christian life pandemic. That is quite a claim. But, while there may be other books on this issue, the scale of the problem within the Church family is still deeply disturbing. I am therefore thrilled that Martina has put pen to paper so powerfully, and on such an important subject as our true identity in Christ.

Intimacy has come to the fore in recent years and challenged the more traditional attitudes about our relationship with our heavenly Father, so that we can experience him more as a God of love. While intimacy is an essential joy in our 'sonship' through Christ, it sits firmly and squarely on the foundation of our identity. Any weakness in our identity foundations will diminish our experience of intimacy. Our understanding of who God is and therefore our identity in Him, directly impacts how we will relate to him. Martina speaks forcefully into this important area of warfare, proclaiming life-changing biblical truths.

One of the significant aspects and major benefits of this book is Martina's inclusion of many helpful and relevant stories from her life to illustrate and demonstrate her teaching. I have been impressed how vulnerable and honest she has been with experiences that are both pointed and painful but also of great benefit to the reader. The danger of the perfect preacher is that we cannot relate to him. That is not the case with Martina. I am sure you will be able to personally relate to many of the real-life stories in these covers and draw much strength and hope from Martina's journey.

Another feature I thoroughly appreciate about this book, and the previous one, is the practical approach and application to all the teaching. Martina's clear heart is to see the five identity traps broken in our lives and the biblical truths change our experience of God. She cleverly uses the twelve spiritual truths in her previous book, to illustrate the damage done by a poor identity and the truth released through a biblical identity. We are promised that if we hold to Jesus' teaching, we will know the truth and the truth will set us free. This is not a book to just read, it is one to be lived and lived to the full.

As with the first book in this series on 'Unexpected Warriors', it provokes us to embrace the unbelievable status and supernatural experience of being Sons and Daughters of God. Unexpected Warriors are those who suddenly find themselves chosen, equipped and commissioned by God, because God has chosen the things that are not, to nullify the things that are[1]. So, to conclude and stay within Martina's continued spiritual allegorical use of the spine, I believe this book cries out to all of us in the Church family, "Grow a backbone". So let us shout together, "Can these bones live? Yes, they can!"

—MARK ILES
School for Prophecy

[1] 1 Corinthians 1:26-31

INTRODUCTION

'I will give you the keys of the kingdom of heaven; whatever you
bind on earth will be bound in heaven, and whatever you loose
on earth will be loosed in heaven.'
MATTHEW 16:19

It was as though somebody had pressed a pause button on life.

Like floating in a warm space between waking and sleeping, yet still being sharply conscious.

The Bath City Church auditorium lights, bright behind my eyelids and refracted through the water, amplified a sense of heaven. An extraordinary peace flooded my soul. No words in my head. Only the sense that beneath that water, it was as though I was completely alone, yet fully immersed in a very safe presence beyond myself. I belonged in that presence. I wanted to stay there.

A tugging on my arms forced me to re-engage my brain and legs. I shot back up out of the water, arms in the air, glinting droplets flying, to cheers and clapping resounding across the auditorium. In that split-second beneath the water, I'd let go of every scrap of old DNA and publicly marked my real identity as a child of my loving heavenly Father.

For a moment, as I looked out at the crowds, my family amongst them, I recognised that I was only at the start of a new journey that was going to be demanding, challenging, and yet the most fulfilling I'd ever embarked upon. St Augustine[2] said that sacraments, such as full-immersion baptism, are 'an outward and visible sign of an inward and invisible grace'. This is so. The inward and invisible grace had been at work in me, and He would carry that forward to completion.[3]

Climbing from the baptism pool, led away for ministry, I dried on the towel draped around my shoulders by my husband. The musicians on the stage struck up, 'In Christ Alone'. The gospel is so simple.

Yet I entered a process that involved laying down my old ways of thinking, mindsets, and habits, and then learning new ways. I was genuinely changing from year to year on a fast yet long track into my real identity in Christ, something that my heavenly Father had always wanted for me and wants for you too.

My first book in the *Equipping Unexpected Warriors* series, *The Posture Principle*, covered what I discovered I had to do first on this journey: focus in on who God really is, establish that internally, and look toward the finish line. In that book, I began to describe the importance of an intimate relationship with a loving God, the God who created us as His sons and daughters, made in His likeness.

In my second book, *The Identity Key,* I share my honest experiences concerning five life-stealing traps or mindsets that hindered full access to my identity as a new creation in Jesus Christ. Our identity in Christ is what unlocks the fullness of our inheritance in God. I replace the five traps with five biblical principles.

I continue to use the biblical imagery of the body of Christ, specifically the lumbar spine, in this book. Each principle is one of five

2   Also known as Augustine of Hippo (13 November 354 – 28 August 430 AD), whose writings influenced the development of Western philosophy and Western Christianity.

3   Philippians 1:6

lumbar vertebrae, working from just below the ribs, down into our hips. I offer practical ways to strengthen them, and therefore our core.

In each chapter, you will find two lists to help you implement the message and lessons of the chapter in your own life. One applies the specific mindset tackled to the twelve spiritual vertebrae from *The Posture Principle*. This demonstrates its destructive effect on them. The other applies the replacement principle recommended in that chapter. This shows the strengthening effect.

I then use three keys: Reflect, Activate, and Question.

A false identity weakens our core. Our core is where our strength lies, it is, therefore, not surprising that it is a key battleground.

My prayer is that the spiritual and practical suggestions I make will empower you to connect the dots of your own life. There is so much more!

May you be inspired to go on your own journey, to move into all that God has for you, and be equipped to help others to do likewise.

> '...to equip His people for works of service, so that the body of Christ may be built up until we all reach unity in the faith and in the knowledge of the Son of God and become mature, attaining to the whole measure of the fullness of Christ... speaking the truth in love, we will grow to become in every respect the mature body of Him who is the head, that is, Christ. From Him the whole body, joined and held together by every supporting ligament, grows and builds itself up in love, as each part does its work.'
> EPHESIANS 4:12-13,15-16

FROM PERFORMANCE TO ACCEPTANCE

'I do not accept glory from human beings...'

JOHN 5:41

CHAPTER ONE

THE ACCEPTANCE VERTEBRA

'Grace means there is nothing we can do to make God love us more... And grace means there is nothing we can do to make God love us less... Grace means that God already loves us as much as an infinite God can possibly love.'

PHILIP YANCEY
What's So Amazing About Grace?[4]

Recently, I hit a week when I was completely exhausted. There seemed to be no reason for it; I'd been feeling fit and healthy and working well.

My son James, a physical training instructor, happened to be staying that weekend. He asked me how my training had been going. I run and walk each day for my cardiovascular health. I told him that I was following my Garmin watch for my heart rate, but that despite running up a long hill three times that week, my status remained 'unproductive'!

Taking my watch from me, and asking me a few questions about my body, whilst doing some sums, he looked carefully at the settings. To my, and his, horror, my Garmin watch had set my maximum heart rate way above that which it should be! Its calculations had me trying to train far too hard for my age, and I was consistently not reaching the goals it had set for me.

I had over-trained. My body was complaining. After weeks of this, it was finally telling me to stop and rest... and change my routine!

Having now reset my watch, it shows a much more sensible assessment of my exercise, within the right zones, to the most effective levels; I am now meeting the goals and my morale has improved dramatically! Now, I will be able to improve my fitness progressively, with a good plan, which will include rest days too. And another tip my son gave me: always listen to your body. I knew that already, but somehow that knowledge got lost in the activity. Never train hard when you are tired. Rest. Take it easy on your body, and do something gentle or different, perhaps muscle-strengthening exercises!

This is a perfect example of the problem with performance. If we are consistently setting ourselves far too high a target, day by day, one day we will crash. This is something so close to our heavenly Father's heart that He has given us a rest day every seventh day. Even He took it! He also recommended we take several days sometimes! The Israelites had many feast weeks throughout the year. They celebrated hard, they rested well.

We are called to be people who carry God's presence everywhere we go. In my first book,[5] I sought to help you focus on the main thing—the One—God Himself. With a mind distracted in all different directions, overloaded by fear of what others think, and pursued by performance demons, we are not going to be able to do that!

---

5   *The Posture Principle: A practical guide to embracing your true calling.* Book 1 of the series: *Equipping Unexpected Warriors.* This is Book 2.

The lumbar vertebrae are the largest segments of our spine. They support the weight of the body, and permit movement. They are created in each of us to carry specific loads. With over-training and heavy load-bearing, we can be at risk of causing them damage or misalignment. On the other hand, if we do not exercise and our core muscles are weak, the same thing may occur.

There is a godly balance to our lives, and God knows how much we can bear. He is specific about the requirement to exercise our core principles; that means reading His Word, allowing it to go from head to heart, and then shaping our lives by it. Putting these things into practice will cause impressive growth, as we learn to discern the good from the bad. Life is a journey, and on that journey, He asks us to talk to Him and gives us His Holy Spirit to show us His ways. He wants us to listen for His particular 'balance' in our lives.

Knowing His acceptance is truly foundational, and this makes it such an important vertebra. It is why I cover it first in this book.

The Snare of the Fowler

Sometimes, we are not aware of the presence of the performance mindset in our lives. We have our smart watch set wrongly. Perhaps, we were brought up with expectations beyond our capabilities and, not understanding that we are unique, we have striven to attain that which is not ours to achieve. Goals others have set for us, we have taken as our gospel.

The performance mindset is rooted in the fear of people and their opinions, not in awe and honour of God. Awe of God brings worship and praise into our hearts, honouring a God who loves us as His children. Looking to Him first for our answers, our protection, and His guidance, is what we are created to do.

When we fly into the trap of performance, we are like a bird caught in a bird-catcher's net. We are trapped and our wings may get broken in our effort to escape. This is the 'snare of the fowler' as described in the Bible.[6]

We may recognise it within our hearts. Let Jesus come, and gently remove the net from your wings as you read.

We may be perfectionists, always working to get things to a place where we can be satisfied—'satisfying the inner critic', as I have heard this called previously. Oftentimes, it is indeed only ourselves who are judging.

Or we may feel and be responding to rejection. Perhaps what we have done, or even who we have been in the past, has not been acceptable to the most important person or people in our lives. Truly understanding our acceptance by God provides true release and healing, and to achieve this understanding, our own identity offers the key.

The problem with a performance mindset is its focus, motive, and result. Spiritually, it is a crusher.

A performance mindset encourages us to depend on ourselves, not on the sacrifice of Jesus Christ. It is personality-driven, not kingdom-orientated. It grows and develops out of poor teaching and of being in an environment where proving ourselves in church, for example, is seen as important. But first and foremost, the seeds are frequently planted in childhood.

A performance mindset comes out of what is called an 'orphan heart'.[7] An orphan heart says that we trust no one, and we must perform to be accepted as good enough. The problem is that it directly undermines the payment Christ made for us to be good enough in Him.

It is, in fact, anti-Christ on the serious end, working for ourselves

6   Psalm 124:7; Proverbs 14:27

7   Read Mark Stibbe's, *I am Your Father*, (UK: 2010) for in-depth detail on the orphan heart and its effects, including performance.

not in faith by the grace and truth of Jesus' sacrifice paid.[8] It is not the gospel. Jesus died to release us from mindsets such as these. It is deeply connected to the religious spirit, which needs saying, as Jesus warned us about it.[9] Not only does the performance mindset bring another kingdom other than God's into situations and environments, including the church, it works like yeast in dough in that a small amount can cause great growth of unintended and ungodly competition and jealousy.

We have the command from Jesus to seek God and His kingdom first.

These are hard truths. Yet the truth is what sets us free when we apply it in our own lives.[10]

Our Repertoire

Many of us have a performance repertoire that comes from our upbringing and our history, which affects the way we live now. Our repertoire, the thoughts and habits that we regularly perform in a day, say much about what we believe, and our mindset.

Habits—formed by daily repetition, good or bad—can be changed! What are we in the habit of doing? How do our thoughts progress throughout the day, and what flows immediately into our mind on waking? Asking these questions at periodic intervals is both revealing and helpful. Then, once we are aware of our negative tendencies, bit by bit, piece by piece, day by day, we can change.

We are, in fact, on continual public display. As it is meant to be as a Christian—our light is to shine, which means we are to be seen! It

8   Ephesians 2:8-10
9   Matthew 23:5-7, and the whole of Matthew 23
10   John 8:31,32

just depends on how we perceive that and act it out. Does our outward appearance on the stage of life match our inward truth?[11] Or are we a character in our own carefully written play?

To discern this, we can look at the fruit.[12] What are the proceeds, the fruit, the profit, from our public display, the performance of our daily lives?

The main meaning of the verb *to perform*, is to 'carry out a task', a function. The second meaning is to 'entertain an audience by acting', singing, playing, and so on. Each such display is a performance. Daily life is supposed to mean, being who we are, in relationship with God and others, carrying out what we see the Father doing.

There are times when we will need to fulfil our calling by being on an actual stage, perhaps genuinely in our role in the visual arts, or in church. The prophetic ministry is just such an area and can be full of pitfalls as a result. This is why it is very important to understand the problem with having a performance mindset and to have trusted advisors around us. I have found enormous benefit in being a part of the School for Prophecy[13] for the last seven years, working and training in a team alongside others who will speak truth to me.

There is a difference between a genuine performance, and the performance mindset. It is the latter that I am writing about. What we really want in our genuine performance, is to be real, without a mask, to the best of our abilities. The performance mindset will not allow that because it will want to cover stuff up and project a more polished image. Yet we, who fall into that trap, are shooting ourselves in the foot because it is vulnerability and truth that really capture people's attention and hearts.

---

11 Matthew 23:28; Luke 11:39

12 Matthew 7:17,18

13 Go to *www.schoolforprophecy.com*, (last access: 10th August 2020), where you will find courses and manuals and a contact to help you. You can be linked with a prophetic school area.

It is crucial to train ourselves to remain stable whether we receive praise or criticism. If we are elated by the praise of others, we can be flattened by their criticism. The key is to know our identity, to understand who we are in Christ. This is what gives us an unshakeable foundation to give praise to Jesus, and look at criticism in order to learn from our mistakes. That is how we grow.

Performance Mindset and the Prophetic

Although I have been involved in the prophetic and spent time in connection with and learning from others involved in this ministry, it was not until I started being regularly taught in a specific school for prophetic training[14] that I really had the right support to tackle my performance mindset, as well as the other traps mentioned in this book.

My mentor[15] introduced me to his school when I began my mentorship in 2013, and it has really been through his training that I have learnt, on repeat, the importance of speaking only for 'an audience of One'. Our lives, our ministry, are for God. I knew this. Yet we need significant others—people who will speak regularly into our lives—to stand with us as we walk the journey.

We are to be real, and focused on God, not on our performance.

Jesus said, 'Seek first the Kingdom of God'.[16] Not only is this a command to worship God first above all—it comes from a good Father. He knew that this was best for us. It lessens the stress. He does not give us anxiety, but peace. He knows that when we focus on Him, we

---

14 School for Prophecy, as mentioned above, *www.schoolforprophecy.com* (last access: 10th August 2020)
15 Mark Iles, leader and founder of School for Prophecy; prophet, teacher, mentor.
16 Matthew 6:33

receive His peace in deeper measure, and we learn to walk with Him in deeper relationship. It is supernatural!

Fruit or Fortune?

It is important to look at the fruit. From the fruit, we see the root. The proceeds of the performance mindset are certainly not relationship. Publicity, fame, self-effort, overwork, tiredness, stress, in the end, are the fruit. Fortune, wealth, and happiness are what the world seeks, whereas the kingdom that the sons and daughters of God seek is far beyond all that. Our inheritance is much greater, and it requires working out of rest, in relationship. The fruit of that, is peace.

The outworking of the performance mindset also manifests in more subtle ways. In false humility, for example, putting on masks to gain approval. This ultimately bears the fruit of deception. Real humility is a right estimate of our worth and value, of who we are in Christ. It is comparing ourselves only to that which God intends for us to be, and allowing both ourselves and others to shine.

When we live in the performance mindset, we act out, and we are often unaware that we are doing so. There is a lack of integrity between who we are publicly, and who we are privately. Oftentimes, there is deep insecurity inside us, that we won't be able to do something well enough and, therefore, we must work harder.

Underneath it all, as I have mentioned, the performance mindset is driven by fear. This is an extremely negative driver. But it can be replaced. All things are possible in God, and He has promised us life in abundance,[17] which we cannot experience when we strive—rather, the opposite happens, and our enemy comes to 'steal, kill and destroy'.

Its replacement, the biblical core principle of *Acceptance*, becomes

17   John 10:10

the first vertebra of our spiritual lumbar spine. This vertebra in the physical world is positioned at the top, the point where we twist and turn, bend and flex. On the same level with the ninth rib and certain vital internal organs, it provides both protection and, from a spiritual perspective, motivation.

Biblical Acceptance

Acceptance is an extremely valuable commodity in a friend. It is of even greater value when we eventually understand that it is what God gives us, and that Jesus describes us as His friends. He expects us to pass that acceptance on to others. If we act on His instruction to love others just like we love ourselves, then that is where we need to start: right at home with ourselves!

If we wish others to accept us, then we must seek our Father in heaven first, for a revelation of who we really are in Him, as His child.

Jesus Christ came to bring us acceptance. He took all of our rejection on the cross. Performance and perfectionism often arise from fear of rejection. We can come as we are to God, who accepts us. We are safe.

This number one vertebra in our physical lumbar spine protects the pylorus,[18] a crucial internal organ, whose name means, 'gatekeeper'. Acceptance by God is our 'gatekeeper'. It is vital in knowing our identity as sons and daughters of God. Just as the pylorus allows food through for further processing, and adjusts the flow of gastric acid, so does acceptance by God allow us to process our lives and attitudes in the light of His goodness.

We have become children of the most perfect Father in the universe. If we have accepted Jesus by believing in Him and His death on the cross, His resurrection, and that He has gone into heaven where He sits

18   The opening from the stomach into the duodenum.

with the Father, then He lives in us, and He accepts us. His Father has become our Father, and our heavenly Father accepts us fully through His Son Jesus Christ. We are sons and daughters of God, and Jesus is our brother! We are adopted into His family. We are given His Holy Spirit as proof.[19]

His Holy Spirit is the wise counsellor, our guide. We are safe in following His instructions because He knows the beginning from the end, and all in between. So when He says rest, we rest; when He says move, we move. He knows and understands how we are made, and Jesus is our great advocate in heaven, constantly praying for us, so I say again—we are completely safe.

Resting in our Acceptance

Our calling in this world is assured when we rest in Him and listen to Him. That is because our calling comes out of relationship, out of grace, out of love, and out of our new nature.

Acceptance has much to do with forgiveness. They are closely linked. We are forgiven of a great debt, and yet so often, we find it hard to forgive both ourselves and others. If we cannot forgive ourselves, we cannot receive God's forgiveness, nor feel accepted. If we cannot receive His forgiveness, then we cannot receive the forgiveness of others toward us —we just don't know how. This means that we are standing outside the acceptance zone, unable to enter.

A major solution then, is to let go of condemnation, which comes from our enemy. Condemnation is designed to drive us harder and harder to get better and better whenever we fail. The solution is to trust God's amazing gift in Jesus and spend time receiving His forgiveness, love, and pure acceptance. Time spent with Him increases

---

19   Please do connect with me if you wish to know more about this at *www.gracecreativity.com.*

revelation, which is a crucial ingredient of the gospel moving from our head to our heart and influencing our actions.

This is such a crucial point, and it is why so many Christian songs carry this message. Take, for example, the opening two lines of the song 'You are my King'[20]:

I'm forgiven because you were forsaken
I'm accepted, You were condemned.

We Are Enough

We become radically free when we realise that we are enough. This is such a simple statement, but one that often takes considerable time and continual effort to fully accept.

We have actually been made perfect in the eyes of our Father God. Jesus gave us His perfection, and that means that we are a completely new creation. If we read through Romans, we can see the effects clearly. The change in becoming new means we no longer need to be tossed to and fro between our old nature and our new nature. Paul makes it very clear, particularly in Romans, chapter eight.[21]

This means that we don't have to perform to be accepted. We are at liberty to make decisions with the Holy Spirit as to what we do and when. As I wrote in my first book of this *Equipping Unexpected Warriors* series, *The Posture Principle*, 'Warriors think for themselves, decide what to believe, and what will drive their life'.

We have a choice. Is it God driving our life, or is it our perfor-mance mentality? A spirit of perfectionism, or the freedom of the Holy Spirit's movement? When we are sure of the Father's love, and of

20   Written by Billy James Foote, originally released by Phillips, Craig & Dean, on *Let My Words Be Few*, (2001)
21   Note particularly Romans 8:1.

the guidance of the Holy Spirit, then we will be free to choose wisely.

The result is that we bear fruit out of our true identity, the one into which we have been reborn.

Warning Signs

Dawn's fingers reached through the curtains. The first birds were already awake.

My neck and head hurt, my body frozen stiff with anxiety pouring through my stomach like acid. My mind began its revolutions, round and round like a stuck record, with no real sound. Blank, unable to think clearly, and fixated on fear.

Sleep once again had played escape and evasion with me, leading me into tense breath-holding and staring at the ceiling much of the night. *I've got to break this cycle*, I thought to myself. It had been ongoing for three months; I'd barely slept a full night.

The start of a warm summer morning; this was the break that I needed. Crawling out of the double bed in the downstairs guest room, which had become my room while we shared our time between our army quarter in Germany and our home in England, I made my way to the coffee machine. Listing in my head the items that needed packing, and checking my watch, I muttered, 'Look after Richard in Afghanistan today, Lord. Keep him safe. Watch over the boys in boarding school until it's time for them to fly to Germany. Help me stay awake while I drive to Germany today...'

Our life was one of to and fro: our sons James and David in boarding school in England for a short time, and Richard away for months at a time serving us and our country. In that period, we needed to keep an army quarter in Germany, at Richard's unit's base, for the brief periods we could see one another when Richard was back from

Afghanistan. For the rest of the time, I remained near the boys in our home in England, so that they could at least spend the weekends with me. Family, for us, was very important.

So I was going to use our home in Germany for the boys' summer holiday. I needed to get away from my duties, from those things that had borne so many sprouts that I was overwhelmed.

I loved spending time with our sons, who enjoyed the outdoors just as much as I did, and developed a deep relationship with them, still ongoing today, through the adventures they got up to. In a way, army life developed our family bonds more, and the holidays we all spent together were times of complete relaxation and fun. There were no mobile phones or emails when they were younger, and most of the time we would separate ourselves from all outside communication. Time together was precious. I believe that is what has kept us a strong family.

In my home village, I had many roles in church over the seventeen years we were members. I'd begun by firmly knowing my task and the value of stillness. This was appreciated and I knew I had something of worth which must not be stretched.

But now I was serving concurrently as an evening house group host and leader, prophetic intercessor, a dancer, a singer in the worship team every Sunday, teacher and host of a daytime group learning how to live in the Spirit, a monthly midweek service leader, a communion server, and more. It was becoming too much, how had I let this happen?

The church had around one hundred and fifty on its electoral roll, and it was the main and largest one, in a group of twelve churches overseen by our vicar. This group of churches was spread throughout villages across the local countryside, some of which had congregations of under ten.

The ordained leadership was stretched across a wide area, and depended on volunteers to make church happen. Our lively and full church in a small village involved a lot of input from only a handful of workers. It meant that those who served were often the ones who took on more.

There were many opportunities in those days and I enjoyed serving. Yet, we also experienced enormous pressure as our church came under criticism from many of the other churches in our group for moving into spiritual gifts and a more modern style of worship. People from other villages started to attend, and became members because they found it more relevant, but this pushed at the boundaries of the traditional village parish system.

I made a regular habit of spending an hour at lunchtime to sit quietly, in the empty church, in contemplation, to be filled again and regain focus. It was essential to my work. Individual people from the village, who did not belong to the church, would, at times, come into the church to be still too, or watch as I practised my worship dance for the next Sunday. They would comment on the healing they felt, or the peace.

This was a joy to us all, and was also a ministry. Yet, I also faced comments from some within the church, that if I was able to spare this daily hour within my work days, I had the time to add more work to my day. The value of silence and stillness with God, and worship of Him in that sacred space fell short of their comprehension. This was my preparation for Sundays when I needed to give what I had received in the week from God, and that needed listening and watching what He was doing.

This is very much like those standing watching the woman breaking the alabaster jar of costly perfume and pouring it over Jesus,[22] who felt that the perfume could have been sold for money to give to the poor.

22 Matthew 26:6-13

They did not see the point she was making, in putting Jesus first.[23]

Service comes out of love, and love comes from being loved by our One and Only heavenly Father. I needed that love and I needed Him to give me the dance moves, and life moves, that came out of being in His presence.

What is crucial to understand, is that the enemy of our soul wants 'more, more, more'. Jesus wants our presence. We carry that presence from being in His presence. That gives us our focus, as I discussed in *The Posture Principle*. We have to know who we are—our identity—and we need to know Who He is and how He sees us, in order to walk in the intimate calling He has for each one of us.

That time which I call 'power-quiet' and focused worship dance was essential to my service. To serve, we need our heart in God, not ourselves. I knew who I was, I knew what I needed. However, the comments played in my mind and whispered to me. When I agreed to go forward for election to the PCC (church council), I should have stepped back from something else. But I let those whispers affect me.

I was duly elected and continued serving the PCC for five years until we eventually left the church. The story can be found in the chapter, *From Unbelief to Faith*.

It was, in fact, a crucial time to serve on the council, leading up to the retirement of our vicar and onward to the appointment of a replacement. We had to bridge the gap, in a period known as an interregnum. The atmosphere was changing, and I was essentially a single mum during much of it, with Richard in Afghanistan, twice over the period, the second time for over a year. I continued taking that time each day, but there was more pressure around it, and I was less able to say 'no'.

---

23 I have spoken in more detail about this in my first book, *The Posture Principle*.

Knowing our identity is crucial. All that is needed is to do what we see our Father is doing. Allowing criticism to sway us, blinds us. Comprehending the way God works and recognising who we are, we can rise above these currents. I was the only mum to my children, the only wife to my husband.

I'd been brought up to please people, to keep the peace. It was as though I'd been programmed to keep everyone happy. Though I had worked for some years on this successfully, it would reappear to influence certain decisions. I had an override switch, that when flicked, moved me into realms outside of my acceptance in God, my identity, and the rest that is to be found in this core relationship. Basically, it meant putting others before Him and moving into striving.

With a leaky valve, the best answer is to simply replace it. Yet, we only seem to realise that when the valve is already leaking far too much. We may not notice the initial drips, or feel that they are significant. But acting swiftly is the answer, or we can end up dealing with a deluge.

Oftentimes, circumstances can exacerbate the problem.

I had experienced twelve house moves in quick succession in this period of our marriage—six of those accomplished alone while Richard was away. We'd lost a child some years before, and I'd suffered the debilitation of M.E. —and then, by the grace of God, its supernatural healing—before attending this church. We'd been through six periods of separation while Richard served on operations overseas. I knew the value of family. I knew the value of health and time.

My heart was in what I was doing; I had a desire to serve God well. Yet, I was on overstretch already. The fact that everyone else was working and serving hard eventually had its effect.

Performance Culture

Living and serving within a strong performance culture is like yeast within dough. It spreads to touch everything. Its roots are in the religious mindset. Whatever I did, however I tried, I could not resist its effect.

When we have grown up in such an atmosphere, we recognise it less easily until we have been trained to spot it. But we can break out of it. With help, we can move out and move on.

Two key factors formed my mindset. Firstly, a constant necessity to 'always be ready'. An army child and then army wife, the grand total of house moves in the first fifty years of my life was thirty, and none of them were our family home until we moved to the village.

Secondly, I was taught to always be aware of what needed doing; a great gift but also a significant habit to break in order to rest fully. *Oughts* and *shoulds* are clear signs of a performance mindset and people-pleasing. Underlying fear becomes a persistent taskmaster. I broke out of the 'oughtery' of my thinking, but I had to face tough choices and carry them through.

Disentangling from the Net

My heavenly Father was telling me that there was a way of being in life that was so totally different to what I was experiencing that it felt like continual rest. Jesus tells us, 'My yoke is easy, My burden is light'.[24] I'd think, 'Actually You know, Lord, it really doesn't feel that way!'

The rescue plan God had put in place came once I had experienced a decline in health, and a holy inner unrest. He began putting people in place, who showed me the alternative and gave me the courage to walk away when it was plain that God was calling us out to new pastures.[25]

24 A crucial passage to live in. Read the whole: Matthew 11:28-30
25 More on this can be found in my chapters, *From Religion to Grace* and *From Unbelief to Faith*.

His plan involved digging into His Word for a fresh understanding of Who He is, letting go of what I thought I understood, and embracing the gospel over again. It meant listening and obeying even when my loyalty kicked in, and when I couldn't understand. His plan asked me to forgive myself and move on. It included walking a seven-year journey of stripping down and building up, a wonderful time of preparation. This is the value of God's type of rescue plan.

The Effects of the Performance Mindset

Let's take a look at how the performance mindset affects the twelve principles, or '*ps*' of my book, *The Posture Principle*.

- Performance tries to run ahead of *possibility* and cannot cope with surprises.

- *Purpose*, in the eyes of performance, is to please by working hard and being perfect.

- The *potential* of performance is overload.

- Performance needs more, more, more *provision*; it cannot be satisfied.

- Performance never feels safe and cannot rest in God's *protection*.

- 'Always be prepared', says performance; it gives no place for God's timing in our *preparation*.

- *Promise* must be grabbed, thinks performance.

- *Prophecy* has to happen NOW for performance; it has to act.

- Performance has to compete; *partnership* becomes synonymous with one-upmanship and drive.

- Oh yes, performance knows *pursuit* very well; but that's *pursuit* of improvement, perfection, praise, fame, wealth...
- Performance believes that *power* lies in striving, not in the rest of God.

Therefore, performance can never be at *peace*.

The Acceptance Vertebra

Now, we will look at how the vertebra of acceptance strengthens those same twelve '*ps*'!

- Acceptance enables us to see the sparkle of *possibility*.
- Acceptance knows we have a *purpose* arranged by God.
- Acceptance brings *potential* out of everything.
- Acceptance has complete trust that God *provides* for every need.
- Acceptance understands we are God's children living under His *protection*.
- Acceptance moves at the pace of our Father's *preparation*.
- Acceptance receives the *promise* of God as unshakeable.
- Acceptance takes time to test, understand, pray through, and receive *prophecy*.
- Acceptance works very well in *partnership*.
- Acceptance recognises *pursuit* is part and parcel of faith.
- Acceptance holds intrinsic value and *power*.
- Acceptance works and lives under the atmosphere of *peace*.

And now, just as the first book in this series had practical 'keys', so I will use three keys in this book: Reflect, Activate, Question.

Reflect

Read the following slowly and imaginatively, and reflect on the feeling, and insights that it gives you:

Imagine that you are watching a video that closely follows the flight of an eagle. A camera has been placed on the huge bird, which enables you to follow its every move through the air, and you almost become the bird. You have an enormous view stretching out far below, and into the distance toward the horizon. You are weaving in and out of rocky pinnacles at the top of mountains, at a speed that makes you dizzy. No carefully planned and mapped-out pathways here. Swooping and diving and soaring and turning, twisting and looping, yet this eagle is fully focused on where it is heading, without concern for what it looks like. No one is telling this eagle what it must do. Regal in flight and appearance, it makes its own decisions and takes responsibility for only what is important in its life. Practiced, perfected, and strong, its flight takes it where it needs to go, with the least resistance and using the wind to power its flight.

Activate

Take a piece of paper or your journal and draw a vertical line down the middle. Then on the left, write any activities or fruit in your life that you consider fit the performance, perfectionism, and people-pleasing category—the three '*p*s' to look out for. On the right, write down those activities and fruit you feel match a sense of freedom in the flight of your life.

QUESTION

Write the answers in your journal, and pray about them.

- »   What is your focus?
- »   Do you feel trapped? Why?
- »   Are you exhausted? Why?
- »   Can you say no? Why or why not?

FROM PUNISHMENT TO HOPE

'We have this hope as an anchor for the soul, firm and secure. It enters the inner sanctuary behind the curtain, where our forerunner, Jesus, has entered on our behalf.'

HEBREWS 6:19-20a

CHAPTER TWO

THE HOPE VERTEBRA

'There is no fear in love. But perfect love drives out fear, because fear has to do with punishment. The one who fears is not
made perfect in love.'
1 JOHN 4:18

The sun streamed through the tall patio window glass. I found myself
dreaming of opening the doors and letting the baked sea-tinged air into
the stuffy study. That glimmer of hope quickly dissipated as I fought to
turn my Saturday-afternoon attention to the eyes of the headmistress
on the far side of the large room. Through her glasses, they always
seemed so cold, grey, like the sea at the bottom of Boscombe's cliffs
on a winter's day. She shifted behind her enormous desk.

'Now, Martina.'

I drew my thin, sixteen-year-old body taller in my blue-checked
summer uniform dress, the belt hanging loosely, though it was as
tight as it would go. My white gloves and straw boater lay on my bed
upstairs in the dormitory, hastily cast off following the obligatory

after-lunch walk. Upon returning, our corridor mistress had let me know that I was summoned to the head's study.

Her Bentley passed me on my walk just as I'd bought a refreshing ice lolly with my sparse pocket money. I was very hungry. It was a hot day as I walked down the streets of Boscombe, and it seemed like a good idea. Just as I was peeling the paper off carefully, minus white gloves, to take a great, big, cold lick, I spotted her face peering at me through her windscreen. It hadn't crossed my mind for one minute that this was against the rules, until I arrived back at school.

'You'd just eaten lunch! You were in uniform, AND your gloves were off. I am disappointed in you. I have our school's reputation to consider. I've had phone calls from the locals,' she enunciated carefully.

My mind computed that we were watched and reported on by the locals...

'Pure greed!' she announced with finality, dismissing me. Her overweight dog chased me out.

I was shamed to my core. I could have laughed, if it weren't so sad. *Greed. Really?* As I stepped cautiously round the forbidden central-hall carpet, I knew that I wasn't greedy. I recognised what had just happened as unjust and pointless, a guilt-trip with no way out. Yet this episode demonstrates clearly, in a very minor way, the problem with punishment and its distancing effect.

Rules and Regulations

That central-hall carpet was another potent sign of rules and punishments that had no real justification apart from the traditions and hierarchy of the institution, or the formation of a false image of what it was to be ladylike.

This carpet starred in a recent message from a former pupil, 'I'm sure

we all have fond memories… Who remembers central-hall carpet?!'
It was the demise of many a girl carrying stacks of books, trying not
to run to the next lesson whilst avoiding oncoming traffic. The hall
was mid-way between two long corridors. Exit and entrance points,
in particular, posed problems with pupils backing up into others, to
allow a teacher through. Hierarchy was demonstrated through the rule
that teachers and parents were permitted to walk across the carpet.
Detention was meted out if we did.

Passing the dining room before heading back upstairs I remembered
the tough liver full of tubes and strings lying on my plate that lunchtime,
and nearly threw up. The others would tell stories of opening fridges
and finding that the liver had wrapped itself around the milk bottle…
as you do on a wet day in boarding school. I almost believed them.

Food was sparse and not always pleasant. I did not want to feel
ungrateful, so I never made a huge fuss. Yet, the one cook who dared
to buy more and feed us well for one term lives on in my memory,
her warm smile across the counter with a tinge of pity as she offered
me seconds.

Our weigh-in every term revealed that I did not find it difficult
to lose over a stone from my already underweight, growing, body.
Besides, no law had been passed against buying an ice-cream, nor
against eating one in school uniform on a very hot day.

The rules and punishments revealed a pettiness, and a lack of way
out, often not matching the perceived crime. The goal was correction
without relationship and guidance. Discipline is different; it is pro-
portionate to the offence, weighing carefully and fairly the gravity
of the transgression, and giving hope, and a way out. Its purpose is
connection, and growth.

I was not rebellious by nature. I also had internal common sense.
How would you have felt in my shoes in that study? Of course, how

we react depends on our background and personality and how strong our identity is, which is why the punishment mindset is included in a book called *The Identity Key*.

Truly knowing our identity gives us hope. I am encouraging us in this chapter to see *hope* as the second vertebra in our spiritual lumbar spine. This is because discipline always brings hope with it—hope of improvement and growth. Punishment does not, it brings fear. When we know who we are, and what we are here for, the punishment mindset loses its power.

Seeking Connection

Good discipline brings the relationship closer, rather than spinning away fast from one another. Discipline comes from a loving heavenly Father, toward His sons and daughters to help them understand that consequences come from mistakes and misdeeds. Discipline points us towards the right path; it shows us how to make amends. Discerning clearly, we will quickly spot a heart that deeply cares about us. Discipline is no fun at the time,[26] but it is worth it.

Punishment is about imposing a penalty on someone for an offence. It inflicts a penalty as retribution. Retribution is connected with vengeance. It is not about redemption.

Punishment is often meted out by people, who are more concerned about preserving their reputation or the reputation of an institution, than they are about helping the person they are punishing, perhaps unwittingly. This can be anyone: our boss at work, our headmistress as in my story, or even a parent. We too can develop a habit of judging and punishing and pass it on to others who look up to us, and down the generations.

26 Hebrews 12:11

The writer of Hebrews in the Bible says that we are not sons of God if we don't receive discipline. We will feel that! There is an inner need for direction and help because we were made for relationship and connection. Without discipline, we are like a rudderless ship heading for the rocks. We need feedback and caring discipline to stay on course.

The problem is that punishment alienates, and it most often makes the underlying issue worse, assuming bad motives and pronouncing guilt without much communication. It labels, condemns, and harms. When meted out for very minor offences, attacking the personality and character of the one we are correcting, it can cause long-term harm, shame, and emotional stunting.

Discipline, on the other hand, seeks connection. Done out of relationship, in kindness, it helps us adjust our behaviour where we have made a mistake or been blind. It communicates before judging. It is fair, helping us to face our consequences with wisdom and transformed mindsets. It seeks to help us own up, learn from our mistake, and make changes to our lives that put the learning into practice. Discipline only deals with what is necessary; it is not small-minded, and it flows out of care for the person concerned.

The kind of atmosphere that true discipline brings is connection, peace, and correction in an atmosphere of love. That releases us to behave with wisdom, learn to handle ourselves well, and develop habits through practising good decision-making daily, hourly even; it gives us hope. There is no fear attached.

I've shared my simple ice-cream story, as it illustrates the concept really well. The issue that brought such a character-debasing interview with my headmistress was minor. But it resulted in long-term effects and relational consequences at school, with perceptions held about who I was as a person. The minor offence was connected to my identity, which gave an impression of being a bad person, shameful, and unable to behave well.

Living in a punishment culture affects our character and who we really are. It blinds us to what God says about us. It has very real potential to destroy our lives.

Why would I like us to look at it? Because it is far too prevalent, in my experience, in families, churches, businesses, and everyday life.

The Death of Intimacy

The biggest problem with punishment is that it destroys intimacy, our self-confidence, and our ability to relate as a person. It breaks down our sense of trust. Trust promotes hope. As a reaction to punishment, we develop masks and barriers.

Consider the headmistress and her relationship with me. I left that study knowing that I had her disapproval looming over me. There was no solution nor hope given. Though the offence had been very minor, her attitude was cold and unforgiving, and I was not to come back—there was nothing more to say. I began to lose my trust in her.

Though I knew full well that what I'd experienced was both unfair and not worth my worry, the incident had the consequence of heightening my performance mindset. I set my heart on proving her wrong, and eventually received the 'deportment badge', a blue metal strip pinned to my front for the year, presented on Speech Day, in front of the whole school and all the parents. *My triumph?* Many would say, 'look how she has improved!' But the reality was different.

It carried a high price. How I carried myself, how I conducted myself, depended on approval from the wrong source. It was not driven from within, but imposed by punishment—and this punishment was of a manipulative kind, using labels such as 'greedy' to change my actions. This label was able to creep into my mind, attacking my self-esteem and affecting my eating habits and health in the upcoming years. It changed the way I thought about myself.

The little lie was so insidious that it almost prevented me from writing about it in this book. I hope that including it will free others, who have felt shame about how they have been described at school or at home... because testimony sets others free. The issue of bulimia and anorexia is a huge one in our society.

Under punishment, we feel condemned and never able to move on. We have no focus or goal given to us except to do better next time or perform. We come under legalism and slip into religious behaviour and habits. Shame becomes our driver. Fear is our taskmaster in the prison of punishment. We carry a great responsibility as leaders, to empower and influence our people, and bring the good out in them, particularly in schools, within our families, and at work.

A Major Life Question

'Here is the major life question: Does our experience create our identity... or does our identity create our experience?'

—STEVE BACKLUND[27]

Steve Backlund trains those who work with him in Igniting Hope Ministries, and as a leader in Bethel Church, Redding, California, to develop a culture of empowerment. In his own life and ministry, he empowers those around him to fulfil their own calling. His book on the culture of empowerment[28] describes his methods of training people

27   Steve Backlund, *Igniting Hope Ministries and Bethel Leaders Network Associate Director.*
28   Steve Backlund, *The Culture of Empowerment: How to Champion People,* (US: 2016).

up, what he expects as a leader, and how to discipline, and mentor. The fruit is plain for all to see, in changed lives and in the empowered people all around him.

As Steve's quote so clearly suggests, bowing to our past history, prevailing world systems, and present ungodly cultures, will create a different reality to living out the truth of our identity in Christ. Living out of our identity in Christ takes a different mindset, but it is the key to creating a kingdom experience, rather than repeating the old record. It takes godly beliefs.[29]

It is around this question that most of my learning experiences during mentoring have centred. Do I allow my past to influence who I am now? Or do I recognise who I am in Christ, behaving and ministering out of that identity? In order to do the latter, we need to, as my mentor[30] always said, 'go weeding!'

The Sword of Damocles

When we are pandering to a punishment mindset, it is like having a huge sword hung above our head, connected by a simple, thin thread. The connection—that of a tentative relationship—is easily broken by the punisher because it is dependent on behaviour. Good behaviour, and it remains unbroken; bad behaviour, and the sword comes crashing down to sever our character and personality, our hope, and wellbeing.

Let me tell you the history of this phrase in brief. Damocles was a fawning courtier to King Dionysius II of Syracuse, a 4th century BC tyrant. He wanted to taste how it was to have such luxurious surroundings and be attended on by all the other servants. His king allowed him the privilege for one day, but hung a huge sword above

---

29 For some focused beliefs training, visit *www.ignitinghope.com* (last accessed, August 2020).

30 Mark Iles, leader and founder of School for Prophecy; prophet, teacher, mentor. His website: *www.schoolforprophecy.com* (last accessed, August 2020)

the throne, connected only by a single hair of a horse's tail. Looking up that evening during a banquet, Damocles noticed the sword and immediately lost all taste for the luxuries. By this, the king who had many enemies, showed Damocles the constant fear in which he, the king, lived.

The expression, 'sword of Damocles', describes living in a state of impending doom. Unfortunately, my life experience had created this underlying sense. This sense was particularly heightened when I had to make important decisions. This is the effect of living life in a punishment culture.

When we finally realise that we no longer need to live there, it is immensely freeing.

The Power of Hope

The power of hope overcomes every mistake. If we have developed in an atmosphere of punishment, rather than discipline, it is an important area to allow our heavenly Father to touch first.

It will need careful healing by stepping out of any punishment environments and relationships, and by setting ourselves free from such a mindset through the power of the Holy Spirit. It will also need the support of strong, committed friends, and maybe ministries like Sozo.[31]

Ongoing mentoring by a kingdom-minded mentor, or even a trusted friend or advisor, brings long-lasting fruit, through being in an atmosphere that brings the truth of God's Word. Spending time in places that are known for their kingdom mindsets and worship, making sure that your church has such a culture, and finding friends to support you in this journey are invaluable.

---

31   *www.bethelsozo.com* (last accessed, 9th August 2020). Bethel Sozo is an inner healing and deliverance ministry.

Reading and meditation on God's Word, looking at it with fresh eyes and an open heart to the Holy Spirit's prompting is essential. Allowing our heavenly Father to touch our hearts in silent contemplation, or during soaking (relaxing with worship music), brings transformation and release, even when it may feel as though nothing has happened.

Through these steps, we will be able to begin truly holding to the truth of Jesus' teaching. Jesus gave a condition to two promises. That condition was, to hold to His teaching to truly become His disciples. That is, to get it under our skin, into our heart from our head, to be like a bulldog keeping it between our teeth, in our mouths, whatever happens. Allow the fresh air of His kingdom to blow out the noxious fumes of a punishment mentality and religious thinking. Then His two promises follow: we will know the truth, and that truth will set us free! [32]

It is the hope that God gives, by His Holy Spirit, through His Word, trusted advisors, and through His personal interaction with us, that sets us free. Punishment keeps us where we are or pushes us backwards.

The Sword of Truth

Fatherly discipline, when needed, comes with God's truth. The Bible actually tells us that we are not His children if we are not disciplined as sons,[33] so when we realise He is bringing something to our attention, simply go with it, speak with Him, ask His Holy Spirit to reveal more to us, and ask for the solution. Discipline has hope attached. Thank Him for the opportunity to grow. Once we know we are communicating in a new way with our heavenly Father, then we will find that we are

32   John 8:31-32.
33   Hebrews 12:8

making our decisions with Him, with ease. Patience and trust will grow.

Our Father knows our heart better than we do.[34] He can tell when we are serious. He will transform and complete His work in us.[35] That is His promise. His Word is a sword, described as cutting even between 'bone and marrow,'[36] and it reveals everything that is helpful for us to see.

The 'sword of truth', or the 'sword of the Spirit' is something given to each of us as part of our armour.[37] Sharpened and polished in the secret place with the Lord and His Word, it may be wielded to cut away lies, accusations, condemnation, misinformation, and any kind of attack by our enemy, the devil. This replaces the sword of Damocles!

It can also be wielded on someone else's behalf. When the Holy Spirit directs, only at the times He commands, in the right heart and with kingdom motives, we may help someone we know to see what they are doing. We may need to speak the truth in love to them. The truth needs honing by prayer and insight, it needs accurate and clear application, and it requires a heart that is in the right place with God. It also needs a bridge of relationship. It is not something to be done lightly or often.

Discipline needs truth and always seeks connection.

My experiences of the culture of honour[38] at Bethel Church in Redding, California have been particularly helpful. This quote by Danny Silk[39] sums up discipline versus punishment well (see following page):

34 Romans 8:26

35 Philippians 1:6

36 Hebrews 4:12 NKJV

37 Ephesians 6:17

38 Read Danny Silk's *Culture of Honour* (US: 2009).

39 Danny Silk serves on the Senior Leadership Team of both Bethel Church in Redding, CA and Jesus Culture in Sacramento, CA. He is the President and Co-Founder of Loving on Purpose.

'Living with humans is messy... Messes are scary, painful, and offensive. And whether we're dealing with the pain of a personal failure, the frustration of a disrespectful child, the devastation of a major betrayal, the stress of a workplace conflict, or the fallout of larger social injustices, classically we react the same way, with fear, shame, and punishment. These reactions are understandable... but they don't do anything to fix the problem. In fact, they only perpetuate a culture of fear, unforgiveness, retribution, and disconnection. Jesus came to show us a better way to respond to human messes, the way of repentance, reconciliation, and restoration. This way removes fear, shame, and punishment from people's lives, empowers them to deal with the root of their problems, and equips them to build a new lifestyle of walking in the light and protecting connection with God, themselves, and others.'

The 'Nice' Need

Discipline takes time and effort. The fruit of godly discipline is luscious and well-formed. Our heavenly Father will show us when we are moving away from His purpose. My experience has been, that hope, our vertebra in this chapter, has always been offered at the same time, though sometimes it may not feel like that![40] There is always choice.

We are the 'Body' of Christ for good reason. The Body works best when we each value one another in love and listen to each other.

Yet, it is impossible to grow in Christ to the maturity that He has provided for the Church, if we have the 'nice' need. It may seem so much easier to be nice, but it so quickly switches to a punishment mindset because problems are buried rather than confronted in a loving manner. Undealt-with frustration mounts until the problems

40 Hebrews 12:11

soar out of proportion. Oftentimes, punishment then follows as a tool to reassert control.

To clarify, it is easy to confuse the word 'nice' with being kind. The meaning behind the words and the intent, are quite different. The Latin root of the word 'nice' actually means 'ignorant'. It only received a respectable meaning in the nineteenth century. Still today it carries a sense of seeking to help a person to feel comfortable in a way that papers over conflict or difficult issues. For the reasons I have given above, this is unhelpful. The godly way forward is to speak the truth in kindness, at the right moment.

Living free, means accepting our heavenly Father's discipline, and that is often through trusted people. I repeat: it is very different to punishment. Punishment leaves us without hope. Discipline guides and corrects our path, and expects us to clean up our messes where necessary. It shows us what the consequences of our actions are and how to walk through to wholeness once more. It is never given in anger, and is always seeking connection. It always, like our heavenly Father, offers hope.

The Good News

There is a reason why our gospel is good news! When we believe we are still sinners, we treat ourselves that way. Unless someone tells us what we are doing, we will continue punishing ourselves and receiving the judgement and punishment of others.

We died 2000 years ago on the cross with Jesus. We need no longer live in turmoil because He set us free. That is what brings the joy of our salvation. Paul in his letter to the Romans, chapter eight, is very clear about this.[41]

I have, however, been present when the opposite has been preached.

41   Romans 8:1-11

I have seen and experienced the effects of such preaching on a church. Not understanding the very clear statement that we are saints, not sinners, opens the way to struggle. The marvellous truth is, we may calmly stand firm on the ground that Jesus paid for.[42] We may hold to His teaching and watch His teaching set us free from struggle.

Jesus promised that if we spend time with Him in the Word, and stick to it in our lives, 'holding' to it like our anchor whatever storms came, then He would impress it onto our hearts, bringing it into our very core, where we will know it, allowing it to become our automatic response in life; it would set us free. We would become His disciples. I can vouch for that. It takes effort. It takes time.

For me, it took walking away and finding Him. It took determination and crying out for more even when I wasn't sure what that would look like. It took healing steps. It took finding a mentor and spiritual father[43] qualified to teach me through a life that proved the truth, and it took his speaking truth into my life for seven years, even when it hurt. It took digging in, growing and learning with my husband Richard, breaking out into abundant life together.

The Effects of the Punishment Mindset

Let's take this mindset and apply it to the twelve life principles I wrote about in *The Posture Principle*. We will see how it brings a negative perception.

- Punishment removes the hope of *possibility*.
- The *purpose* of punishment is to bring others to conform to tradition, religion, institution, or control—to instil fear.

---

42 Ephesians 6:11,13

43 Mark Iles, prophet, teacher, mentor and founder/leader School for Prophecy.

- There is no *potential* in punishment. It is a dead end.

- The *provision* of punishment is living in a trap of performance and fear of disapproval.

- Those who operate out of a punishment mentality are only interested in the *protection* of their interests and honour.

- Punishment takes us by surprise, giving no *preparation* for the damage it causes.

- *Promise* is eliminated by the punishment mindset.

- *Prophecy* spoken out of a punishment mentality is not a New Covenant prophecy.

- The punishment mindset precludes *partnership*. No one in the kingdom wants to work with a religious spirit.

- Pursuing punishment means rejecting our *pursuit* of God.

- The *power* of God is removed in a punishment environment because the punishment mindset is connected to the religious spirit, which has no *power*.

- Those who punish, and those who are being punished, are not in the presence of the *Prince of Peace*.

The Hope Vertebra

Now for the effect of hope on those same twelve life principles!

- *Possibility* in God is genuine, true, hope! Not a hope that disappoints.

- Hope makes investigating our *purpose* in God exciting, not fear-filled.

- Hope expands our *potential* as we dream with God.

- We are told never to be anxious about God's *provision*. Hope brings confidence.

- Hope is a helmet of *protection*—we wear the helmet of salvation, what Jesus did for us on the cross.

- By increasing our hope in God, we are *prepared* as we walk our journey, whether smooth or rough.

- We have a secure hope that His *promise* is sure, that He will complete the work He has started in us.

- New Covenant *prophecy* brings us hope, not discouragement.

- Hope always sees the good in other people, and works in *partnership* to bring the kingdom together.

- *Pursuit* flourishes with hope.

- Never underestimate the Spirit-inspired *power* of hope!

- Hope is eternal, it brings us *peace* as we trust God.

Reflect

Reflect on this quote:

> 'My flaws and failures make me *unworthy* of love, belonging, and connection. I deserve disconnection and punishment. So does everyone else with flaws and failures.'[44]

There is deep shame in this way of thinking. In this place, fear of punishment drives our motives. It doesn't have to be this way.

44 The core belief of the punishment paradigm. Danny Silk, *Unpunishable* (US: 2019).

The second vertebra in the spiritual lumbar spine, the biblical principle of hope, means that no mistake ever made is final. Jesus covered every mistake and failure on the cross 2000 years ago. Our faith tells us that when we believe in Jesus, we were in Him when He died, and we were in Him when He rose and ascended to heaven. Therefore, we are a new creation. The old has gone and the new has come.

Our Father cared so much for us that He sent His only Son to die in our place. But He had a plan! The arch-punisher, the devil, never expected that. When we receive what God has graciously given to us, we have defeated the devil. That is all it takes. Receiving.

On this journey into deeper identity, it is important to reflect on our past, our attitudes, and our habits before we move on. You can take more time with this when you have read the whole book, going back to the parts that have been important to you.

The quality that separates the believer from the non-believer is the knowledge that we have an eternal hope through Jesus Christ. The problem with this is that not all believers know it, nor do they act like it.

Eternal hope means that we are never at the end. There is always a way out with God our Father. Joy is always a possibility because there is always a solution. Mistakes can be learnt from. We are called to have sparkling hope! Our identity is secure in Christ.

Remember that identity is the large key to living in intimate relationship with God, which is our true calling.

Activate

I think, with such a tough subject, our activation needs to be in the opposite spirit. It will be letting go and receiving, in silent worship with music. This is called 'soaking' in God's presence, where He can transform us as we abide. Know that His love, His passion, His goodness, and everything that belongs to Him, belongs to you, and you may receive in this still place.

Lie down, preferably, and relax in God's presence. Have some music playing. Using music is a biblical practice.

The Father is waiting for you. It may have been so long since you have approached Him this way, or never. But His mercy is ready; you just need to receive it. Try to do such soaking regularly because it is in this very place of intimacy and relationship that He can transform you best. Revelation transforms us, not head knowledge.

I have written in *The Posture Principle,* about this as one of the five keys to focusing on God. I use soaking with music as well as times of soaking in complete silence.

QUESTION

Write the answers to the questions below in your journal and pray about them.

» Did God show you anything as you spent time soaking? If so write that down in your journal. It may be that He showed you a measure of His presence far beyond your normal. Record that.

» Is there any area that you need to bring to Him so that you can clear it up with Him?

» Do you understand that He loves and accepts you just as you are? Let Him increase that day by day. It is useful to pin notes on your mirror of verses that express that in order to help this reality sink in.

FROM DUTY TO LOVE

'And yet I will show you the most excellent way.'

1 CORINTHIANS 12:31b

CHAPTER THREE

THE LOVE VERTEBRA

'There are lovers and there are workers. And lovers get more
work done than do workers!'

MIKE BICKLE[45]

The Presence

We sat in what seemed to be complete silence, yet there was a language
spoken between us that needed no interpretation. I didn't recognise
where we were sitting, but it seemed to be a kind of waiting room
allocated only to us. Jesus was on my left, and I was on His right at
an angle so that we could look at each other and communicate. The
surroundings were clinical and white, and we were sitting on white
box benches integral with the floor.

In His presence, peace permeated every cell of my being. I relaxed.
Though I could not see my body, I could see Him. He was in whitish
robe-like garments, like He would have worn in Israel in His days on

---

45   Leader of IHOPKC (International House of Prayer, Kansas City). Quoted by Bill Johnson in *Dreaming
     With God* (US: 2006).

earth. He looked very comfortable. He was sitting companionably, waiting with me. I could not really see the features of His face, but that seemed normal at the time. I could sense Him and understand Him and feel completely secure and at ease with Him.

I want to stay here forever! I thought.

Immediately, Jesus showed me my husband and two boys, who were anxiously waiting for me, wherever they were at the time—at school, and at work. I knew what He was saying. 'They need you'. Love poured into my heart for them.

I said to Jesus, 'I love being with You. But I am going back.'

Immediately Jesus faded, and I heard, 'Martina! Martina! Come on, wake up!' Then, 'Her eyes are flickering...' and I opened them. 'You weren't coming round! We had to give you more anaesthetic to keep you under longer; the doctor will explain. We will just wheel you into the recovery room now...'

And I fell back into the depths of sleep.

What seemed like days later, but was not, I awoke, and opened my eyes. A man was standing by my bed waiting.

'Hello Martina! I'm Mr Angel,'—I am sure I heard Jesus laugh as though He loved His own joke—'I'm the surgeon who operated on you'.

He showed me a small bottle next to my bed, filled with what I could only describe as gravel.

'Unfortunately, your gall bladder burst as we were removing it, and it was filled with gravel, not just one big stone. The gravel flew all over the inside of your abdomen, and we had to hoover you out as best we could. You were under much longer than we expected.'

I imagined the hoover stuck in between all my internal organs...

He smiled and said, 'You can keep this as a memento!' The doctor then told me to rest, and he left the small cubicle.

I was intensely aware of the pain throughout my abdomen, the bruising and the cuts. Groaning I tried to rest and remember the encounter I'd had with the Jesus I loved, who had waited with me, while they tried to wake me. I was incredibly grateful, and there was a sense of wonder because I knew from previous encounters, that He had something very special for my family.

What I knew was that in people with a healthy weight, gallstones can be caused by stress and internal anxiety, particularly if there is an inherited tendency. As Mr Angel showed me his little bottle, I recognised this could be the cause.

The effects of my fears were revealed in that bottle. Yet also I recognised, the empowering, peace-filled presence of Jesus that had been offered to me as a gift.

Eventually, my husband turned up to take me home and take care of me. The year was early 2002. So let me use more of my story to show you how I have moved from a duty mindset to love, and how love has set us free.

Love Sets Free

My husband is the kindest person on earth (at least I think so!).

I am sure that grabbed your attention! It was meant to. For over thirty-five years of marriage and thirty-eight in love, we have grown together as co-labourers on an adventure. During that time, Richard, after university where we met, attended Sandhurst, rose to the rank of major-general in the British Army, chose to leave when we set up our business six years ago, and travelled Africa extensively with the Brenthurst Foundation, as their special advisor.

Two years ago we hit a point, prompted by an event, where we decided that we wanted to spend more time together, both in our work and in our play.

Whilst on my early morning walk, I'd discovered something blocking my vision in my right eye. Thinking it was a piece of fluff I was not overly concerned. However, as it continued and no doctor was available, I went to my optician. He sent me straight to hospital.

I was seen by a trainee consultant at a very busy time and though he sent me for a range of follow-up tests, which included booking me in to have an arterial operation on my right temple the following week, he pronounced a serious, life-changing diagnosis. He handed me a prescription for a top-level dosage of steroids, which he said I would need to take for the rest of my life. I began to quiz him on the latter as I hated the idea of steroids and wanted to know exactly why.

As he was giving me his assessment of the deterioration I would go through, I suddenly began to 'see in the Spirit'. In this vision, in front of me I 'saw' an armchair, and in that armchair sat my heavenly Father, God. All the while that the consultant was speaking, He sat there, looking at me.

I sensed my Father God say to me directly, 'Am I a good Father?'

My memory flashed back to another testimony, this one was my mentor's. He had also had an encounter with his heavenly Father, to assure him that He was in control of the situation and all would be well—and it was. He tells his testimony on his prophetic courses.

I responded immediately, through my tears, 'Yes. You ARE a good Father!' Then, I felt Him tell me to go along with the prescription, just for now, but that it wouldn't be for a long time. I was obedient, and spent two weeks on them, after which I was permitted to wean myself off them. Though the diagnosis turned out to be rather wide of the mark, the steroids kept me from losing any more vision during the time of inflammation. Father knew what He was allowing.

I'd lost the lower half of the field of vision in my right eye. The reason was found to be a rare condition. It led to a full life-style change at home, aimed at preventing further loss. I also had a team of thirty people praying, who supported me at the time! The immediate aftermath involved months of appointments, scans, blood tests, and visits to the hospital.

Richard was immediately given the time off to look after me. It brought our whole decision-making process a lot closer, and we found it led automatically into a brand-new journey. Once again, God stepped into what the enemy meant for harm, to redeem over and above what was taken from me.

Gradually, something that we had never truly experienced began: prolonged times when we were both at home.

We still had different places we needed to travel to, but they were now mainly in England, where we live. In stark contrast to the pre-conceptions of some who have commented on this new phenomenon, we have actually truly flourished in each other's company. It has been a real gift.

Something wonderful developed as this progressed. I would find Richard freely helping me with the housework and garden! This was very welcome. Yet when this happened at times when I hadn't planned it, when I had decided to work in my study or perhaps take some time out, I found myself bothered. I discovered I had a problem.

This period of my discomfort only lasted a few months during the first year. I believe that is because we have a relationship in which we can talk honestly with one another. It was easy to overcome by realising the benefit and that his intention was to free me up to do the new work in which I was becoming involved and to give me time to rest. What a gift. But it was not what I had perceived at first; rather my mind was telling me that I was not doing my job. By talking and being open, we managed to work this through quickly.

I had an automatic switch in me, implanted into me as a child, that pinged every time someone got up to do some work. It would flash red in my mind and shout, 'Alert, alert!' I would need to get up and offer help, or even do it for them. If I remained 'sitting around' whilst my mind continued to accuse me, I'd experience unrest and guilt, and my body would be sending constant distress signals. Why it remained with me was a surprise, for later in life, my mother and father would look after us and have us rest when we visited them with our children. I believe it was a remnant from growing up, a beneficial one, that became over-active, and was probably also linked with my 'responsibility' talent on the StrengthsFinder scale.[46]

My home life experience had also been that women did the housework. Now, my mind did not think that, but in practice, it became evident that I had a faulty belief! Richard had a father who involved himself in the housework and the cooking for much of the time, whenever he was at home. He was used to that way of life.

At times when I heard the vacuum cleaner, I would leap up and say, 'I was going to do that—really!'

He would respond, 'Stop feeling guilty—just accept it!'

My automatic setting from childhood took a while to switch off, and I'd continue to feel the guilt trips working themselves out in my mind as I retired back into my study—or even as I relaxed in my armchair.

This year as I write, 2020, has been both remarkable and freeing for me. It has brought a revolution in how we are working from home, not simply due to the global lockdown caused by COVID-19, but because we have chosen to spend increased time together in our work. I have particularly needed help to do the housework and garden whilst I have journeyed through an intense period of writing and taking part in a

46   Tom Rath, *StrengthsFinder 2.0 – Discover Your CliftonStrengths* (US: Gallup Press, version 2017).

demanding online art course, as well as attending teacher training with the School for Prophecy.[47] It has been a busy period.

But I no longer have the duty mindset. I am entirely relaxed about having help. The one thing I do is retain a grateful heart and speak that out very regularly. We have also worked out a way to co-labour in the house together—checking the balance regularly and ensuring that both of us are fulfilled, particularly as Richard continues his work with our business and his outside roles.

In conclusion to this story, I recognise that Richard has worked out of love, not duty. I have come to understand that his heart has been that way throughout his life-long service. That was one of the qualities I loved about him when we first met. He has not worked out of a duty mindset, rather he has seen what needs doing and done it to the very best of his ability, for people—of whom I am one. He has been an example to me, also, in that he is not afraid to become less to serve more. His love vertebra is strong and growing stronger by the day.

In Disguise

The duty mindset is insidious because it often disguises itself as love. Jesus told us that nothing done without faith pleases God. That means, trusting in a loving heavenly Father, who would like to see us using the gifts, time, and energies He has given us to the best of our abilities. The parable of the talents demonstrates vividly how He feels when we bury our gifts.

We can bury them in dutiful service. In the process of being who we think everybody needs us to be, always there for them, and always available, we are doing our Father a disservice. He simply says, do on earth what you see your Father in heaven doing. At times, that

47   School for Prophecy, URL: *www.schoolforprophecy.com* (last accessed, August 2020).

means walking past what we feel is a duty. Jesus left villages where His disciples felt He should stay, and He focused only on what His Father was doing. Yet, he accomplished an incredible amount in the three years of His ministry. He focused on working out of love.

Jesus often didn't do what those around Him, including His followers and friends, expected. A prime example is when He didn't go directly to the house of Lazarus, Mary and Martha's brother, when they told Him that he was gravely ill. In fact, instead of urgently rushing to His friend's death-bed, Jesus waited for several days before going, as He was always doing only what He saw the Father doing, even if it made no sense to the people around Him:

> *'Now a man named Lazarus was sick. He was from Bethany, the village of Mary and her sister Martha. This Mary, whose brother Lazarus now lay sick, was the same one who poured perfume on the Lord and wiped his feet with her hair. So the sisters sent word to Jesus, "Lord, the one you love is sick." When he heard this, Jesus said, "This sickness will not end in death. No, it is for God's glory so that God's Son may be glorified through it." Jesus loved Martha and her sister and Lazarus. Yet when he heard that Lazarus was sick, he stayed where he was two more days.'*
>
> (JOHN 11:1-6 NIV)

Mary and Martha

I wrote about the story of Mary and the perfume in *The Posture Principle*.

When Jesus visits the home of Mary and Martha in another story, Mary was described by Jesus like this, 'Mary has chosen what is better, and it will not be taken from her.'[48] Mary had chosen to sit at His feet

48 Luke 10:42

during His visit, to hear and understand what He was teaching. He told Martha, 'You are worried and upset about many things, but few things are needed—or indeed only one.'

Mary was listening to Him and imbibing His presence. She was not concerned about those things for which He was not asking. His intent was to teach. Her intent was to learn. Everything else could be done later.

Martha totally missed this point. Her training as a hostess kicked in, missing Jesus' plan. She put her service first. Rather than serving out of His presence, at the time required, she went to work, providing a meal for Him.

The problem with a duty mindset is that eventually it has us releasing frustration towards others who do not see the situation in the same way. Lack of love comes with that, particularly negative fruit such as jealousy. Martha came out of the kitchen and railed at Jesus, 'Why can't you get Mary off her backside to help me look after you? It's not fair that she should be able to listen to you and I can't!' (My own words.)

This is a work-oriented approach to God. Mary's was grace-oriented. The truth is that service automatically emerges out of love. It is just timed differently. Love puts loving first, and it will not be side-tracked from that focus.

We are not called to be either Marys or Marthas—one or the other— and it is not even a matter of balance between the two. The biblical truth is that love and service go together because service is birthed out of love.

Bill Johnson makes a great point in his book, 'Dreaming With God.'[49] He says, 'Mary wasn't a non-worker; she just learnt to serve from His presence, only making the sandwiches that Jesus ordered. Working *from* His presence is better than working *for* His presence.'

This is a major lesson to learn, and it is not an easy one. It took

49 Bill Johnson, *Dreaming With God* (US: 2006).

me years of 'serving' before I realised that much of my serving could probably be burned up as wood, rather than being the precious gold of love.[50]

When we build on our identity in Christ, on our salvation in Jesus, we must build with awareness. Whatever we do will be tested for its value in the end. Building with love-inspired faith and the gold of a true motive, not the wood and stubble of duty mindsets, can never be burned up. Only faith pleases God.[51]

We do not live by the law of duty. We live by faith.[52]

Responsibility or *Response-ability*?

Duty is often defined as 'a moral or legal requirement'. This is something that is binding, obligatory, or required. It holds an expectation from others that it will be fulfilled, and thus includes, in the natural, the pressure to perform. In the kingdom, love must be our motivation.

Duty can be the outworking of the role or function we hold in life, for instance in the military, or as pastors and clergy in the church. It also applies to family roles: husbands and wives, parents to children, for example. But whether these duties are delivered out of love or obligation, that is the key. Duty in itself is not evil or 'wrong', but the issue I am getting at is a duty mindset. There remains a fresh way of seeing duty. I would like to lead us into it.

Learning to assess what we are responsible for and what is not ours to take on is a start. When we say 'yes' to something, we normally have to say 'no' to another thing, if we are to stay away from becoming overloaded.

50 1 Corinthians 3:10-15
51 Hebrews 11:6
52 Galatians 3:11

Through the very helpful StrengthsFinder test,[53] I discovered that one of my top-five 'talents' was what they call 'responsibility'. Talents can be honed to become strengths. However, before we have honed them, they may amplify existing weaknesses. Those of us who are strong on 'responsibility' will know that it is hard to resist saying 'yes' to everything.

This is exhausting. Our energies become dissipated and our focus is neutralised. I tend to concentrate on what I need to do to help others do first, rather than on my own work, which means that I then experience guilt trips over what I have not accomplished within my own life.

We can end up chasing ourselves round the block and back to the start on repeat. Life becomes a marathon of 'to-dos'. The list grows and grows until we don't bother with it anymore because we can't find where we left off last. It can get so bad that we don't even have time to create a list.

One method of considering what we should prioritise as our daily work and the focus of our effort is by working out what it is that only WE can do. Put that first. What is it that no one else, but you, can do? Then, discern what falls within your sphere of responsibility. Perhaps, also discover what you would really love to do, or what Father God has put into your heart as something new. These are simple suggestions to start the journey.

Learning to Work Out of Rest

We live in the 'shoulderies' and the 'oughteries' as my friend Jane describes them. She and I have walked twenty-five years of this journey together, to freedom. Come to think of it, 'shoulderies' incorporates

---

53   Tom Rath, *StrengthsFinder 2.0* (Gallup Press, US: 2007), is a useful resource.

the word 'shoulder', as well as 'should'. When shoulds are on our shoulders, our shoulders become weighed down.

We are created to work out of rest. Our God created us on the sixth day, meaning that the seventh day, our first day of the week, was a day of rest! There is a rhythm to life if we live in God. He speaks, we listen, we know His presence, and then we move. He spoke out our creation, our 'being' was formed, and we rested with Him before we began our work.

I have a couple of books by the freelance trainer and retreat leader Tony Horsfall. One of his books is called, 'Rhythms of Grace: Finding intimacy with God in a busy life.'[54] I have had this book for a number of years; it is written around Jesus' words in the gospel of Matthew,[55] inviting us to come to Him and learn the unforced rhythms of grace. As I read and reread The Message version of Jesus' words, over the years, this idea drip-fed into my deep inner well. Years later, when I encountered Bill Johnson's teaching on hosting the presence of God,[56] and it hit so many chords, I knew that learning this rhythm would be a lifelong process.

Learning to work out of rest has taken hours of digging deep into God. Though I encountered Jesus at the age of five whilst colouring and writing on a picture,[57] it was not until later, at boarding school, that I took another step along the way and confirmed my life commitment to Him. I'd just turned thirteen and my best friend had invited two others from the dormitory and myself, to make a commitment after lights-out, in the corridor, with some Bible verses. The year was 1975.

Immediately, I sensed the Holy Spirit begin to speak to me during

---

54 Tony Horsfall, *Rhythms of Grace* (UK: 2004); the second book: *Working from a place of rest – Jesus and the key to sustaining ministry* (UK: 2010).

55 Matthew 11:28-30

56 A book worth reading: Bill Johnson, *Hosting the Presence – Unveiling Heaven's Agenda* (US: 2012).

57 Described at the start of my first book in this series: *The Posture Principle* (UK: 2017).

those days, and life lifted for me for a while. I would wake early in the morning with my Bible and journal in hand—something I had not been taught by anyone—and write down whatever I thought I was hearing, to put into practice that day. My friend Kate had given me a modern translation, called 'The Way', which had photos of teenagers praying and short sections explaining up-to-date applications of each book in the Bible, with practical advice for daily living.

The very first time I read about going deep to listen and rest in God was when our two boys were toddlers, when Joyce Huggett led me on a journey through her book, 'Listening to God'. At the time, working out how to fit this into a schedule with toddlers was challenging. But the thirst for it within me was strong, and I found the time to go deep.

In Pembrokeshire, on our family summer holidays, when the boys had not yet woken, I would sit on a nearby rock on the top of a cliff overlooking the sea. I will never forget those times, where I could feel God's very close presence and hear Him speaking His rest into my heart, His love, and His power.

It has brought fruit many years later, giving me a firm foundation when things became very rocky.

I tell you this because I believe that reading other people's experiences and gaining their insights gives us vital support and encouragement. Having friends to walk the journey with us is also essential.

For me, the journey has been a long one, and it is not yet finished. Glancing through my bookshelves, I see title after title on this subject, dating from 1992 when I began to seek how to implement this in my life.

My stumbling block came in the form of wanting to please people. Just as how Martha, or those observing, did not understand Mary when she poured expensive ointment onto Jesus, I found there were people who felt—as I have described in my chapter, *Performance to*

Acceptance—that if I was not doing anything, I was being idle. What they did not understand was that the practice I had established in my life was my life-support system! I have learnt to block them out.

The Effects of the Duty Trap

In order to prepare for our reflection, I'd like us to run through the effects of this duty mindset on the twelve principles in my first book.[58]

- The duty mindset stifles *possibilities* with legalistic service.

- The duty mindset tunes out our Father's *purpose.*

- The duty mindset sets our *potential* aside for another day while we look after others.

- The duty mindset stores up the *provision* from God given to them to use until a 'suitable time'.

- The duty mindset bears an underlying fear that it will not have God's *protection* and blessing, if it is not serving someone else.

- The duty mindset buries God's *promise* under a mound of 'oughteries'.

- The duty mindset balances the *prophecy* it has received with the 'shoulderies'.

- The duty mindset serves with an orphan spirit, so that *partnership* cannot be out of relationship.

- The duty mindset *pursues* righteousness by works.

- The duty mindset is *powerless.*

- The duty mindset is never at rest; it cannot find *peace* because it does not serve the Prince of Peace.

58   *The Posture Principle: A practical guide to embracing your true calling* (UK: 2017).

The Love Vertebra

Now, to compare the love mindset and see how it applies to the twelve principles:

- With love, all things are *possible*.

- Love means that each one of God's children, including me, has a *purpose*.

- Our Father God created every man and woman in His image, which means that we were created in love, carrying His unlimited *potential*.

- God loves us deeply and will always give us the *provision* that we need, both for ourselves and others.

- Love always *protects*.[59]

- Love never leaves us helpless; our God will always *prepare* us.

- Love always keeps His *promise*.

- God speaks into our lives about His love, through others in *prophecy*.

- We are called to be a Body living in God's love, working in *partnership* with one another.

- Love *pursues* us.

- The *power* of love overcomes all wrong.

- Love lives in *peace*.

---

59   1 Corinthians 13:7a

Reflect

Reflect on your current life, and how you are aware of His presence. Consider where you feel closest to Him. It could be sitting still in your home, at work, on a walk in the countryside or in the city, in church, wherever.

Sit quietly and read again, first through the Love Vertebra statements above, and then through the Duty Traps. Give time to allow the Holy Spirit to speak through them.

Remember, a branch cannot bear fruit by itself, it must remain attached to the tree.[60]

Activate

Write the Love Vertebra and Duty Traps down on post-it notes, then stick them in prominent places, for instance, on the mirror or your fridge. As you read, they can begin to permeate your soul.

Take a large sheet of paper (A3 preferably) and a pencil. You will probably need an eraser too as you'll find yourself rubbing things out so that you can fit them in more easily, or change their position! Place the sheet in landscape position.

Now draw the trunk of a large oak tree coming up from the bottom and add some branches. Now begin to draw leaves onto branches, each leaf standing for something for which you are responsible, a role you have, or something you do, all your hobbies, your exercise—everything that is filling your life right now, and include your family and friends.

60   See John 15

When you are done, have a careful look. It may surprise you. This will lead you to an assessment of your time, duties, habits and practices, as well as all the interests, hobbies, tasks, and responsibilities you have. You could then create what I call a 'timetable journal', where you list three to five main priorities for each day and have space to make notes about how it went for you. This means you can make adjustments as you learn new time habits. It will help you stay focused and keep 'duty' at bay.

Don't allow this process to dominate, rather let it be a key to help you find more time to rest with God, remove duty, and insert love into your life.

There are so many worship songs about this to listen to, but it is perhaps best summed up in the opening lines of Rita Springer's song, 'Resting (In Your Presence)'[61]:

'Resting in your presence
Is all that I want Lord
Sitting in your presence
It's all I really ask for
I want to be more like you.'

QUESTION

» Do you have a love relationship with God the Father, God the Son, and God the Holy Spirit? That is, do you converse with Him regularly? Would you like to?[62]

---

61 Rita Springer, *Resting*, from the album *Created to Worship*, (2010).

62 If you want to know more about this, please do contact me via my website: *www.gracecreativity.com*.

» How did you feel when I described my encounter with Jesus at the start of this chapter? Talk to Him about it. Ask Him to reveal Himself to you.

FROM RELIGION TO GRACE

'...if you declare with your mouth, "Jesus is Lord," and believe in your heart that God raised Him from the dead, you will be saved.'

ROMANS 10:9

CHAPTER FOUR

THE GRACE VERTEBRA

'I am astonished that you are so quickly deserting the one who called you to live in the grace of Christ and are turning to a different gospel—which is really no gospel at all.'

GALATIANS 1:6-7

The Things of the Spirit

The year was 1994, the year in which there was outpouring of the Holy Spirit in what was called, 'The Toronto Blessing'. Sandhurst Chapel was our church at the time, where we had been married nine years before. We were posted there, for Richard to train on another course.

As a member of the Officers' Christian Union, and of the daytime Ladies Fellowship group, I knew the vicar well.

One day he asked me, 'Martina, my wife has a ticket for the three-day Church Growth Conference at Holy Trinity Brompton, and she can't go, nor can I. Would you like to take her place? That is, if you're willing to give us all a summary on your return?'

Well, how could I say no? I was very excited. My husband Richard arranged for his parents to visit, to look after the boys who were one and three at the time, while he studied for his course. An aunt of his lived in a large house in Chelsea, round the corner from HTB, where I could stay.

I learnt so much, not only how they'd made such strides into a new way of doing, and growing church. We were taught in the many sessions by Nicky Gumbel and Sandy Millar. I especially soaked in the things of the Spirit. I received more than I had bargained for! The Holy Spirit was very active, as they too were being touched by an outpouring like the Toronto Blessing, and I was blessed and equipped through the ministry and seminars. It was where I first received my call to write and to develop my prophetic gifting.

Firstly, I was struck by the worship. I had never seen anything like it, despite my experience at school, when I came to know God in a different way through my friend, a charismatic Baptist. At school, we attended a United Reformed Church every Sunday. The congregation were very kind and welcoming to us, but we sat up in the gallery of the church, dressed in our uncomfortable uniform. I struggled to stay awake until I began to hear the Holy Spirit and found the grace to listen even in the driest of places. That training was invaluable.

After we lost our first child, my husband and I were occasional visitors at the local Anglican church near Maidstone barracks, then after another move we attended a very high Anglican church, in Bushey, near Watford. God was on my case already there as the lady curate was Spirit-filled and worked on me to teach a workshop on the fact that we were not sinners, but saints! I didn't have a clue then, so I declined. I wondered how I could teach on the classic 'Saints', let alone be one! Yet, I have never forgotten her visits and prayers.

After a year-long posting at Shrivenham, where David, our youngest son, was christened, we now found ourselves members of the church at the core of the British Army, Sandhurst Chapel in Camberley.

The services were normal liturgy and mainly aimed at the soldier and serving officer congregation, yet its groups were highly active in the spiritual gifts. By the time we left, I'd enjoyed involvement in more healings and prophetic input than in all my previous years as a Christian, as well as building deep and lasting relationships.

This vicar knew how to manage the tension of tradition that was required in the services, whilst fully supporting and encouraging the power of the Spirit to affect and pervade the college, families, and schools, through us, outside the church. Witnessing and moving in the gifts became normal for me there. The Officers' Christian Union had the green shoots of new life within it.

Now, I was witness to free and exuberant worship at the HTB conference that sparked such a desire in my heart. I was set free on those three days to a deep and lasting level that launched a new life journey, but one which was not at all easy.

Secondly, I received several gifts and impartations. A major, effective one was the gift of tongues, which I had not yet accessed.[63] On return to my room that first night, I asked the Holy Spirit to teach me. I opened my mouth and began to make noises. From that faltering first step of complete childlike trust and desire, began my spiritual language, and I fell asleep speaking it! On return home, it became a major force of spiritual refilling for me, something I could do even when filling the washing machine! It changed atmospheres, gave me insights, and brought God's presence when I felt lacking.

Over the following years, I developed several different kinds of language.[64] I also asked[65] for, and received the gift of interpretation so that when I was praying in tongues, the Holy Spirit would often

---

63   The spiritual gift of tongues is listed in 1 Corinthians 12:10.

64   'Different kinds of tongues' is listed in 1 Corinthians 12:28.

65   1 John 3:21-24; Matthew 7:7

also reveal to me what I was praying.[66] Without this gift, I would not have had the strength to withstand the storms to come.

A significant gift that was highlighted to me during the conference, with hands laid on, was the prophetic. This, I began to develop through reading Graham Cooke's teaching, visiting his conferences, and interacting with my vicars when I sought to implement it. But the real growth and impact of this gift came later with the help of my mentor and his school.[67] This has been, and remains, my main area of ministry.

My Heavenly Father's Plan

Memories from my childhood, like pepper—for instance, a fire-and-brimstone Church of Scotland preacher talking about hell—or on the other hand, like salt—the wonderful Anglican church nursery I attended where I encountered Jesus for the first time—are scattered throughout my history.

My family did not attend church consistently, in fact this used to be a rare occurrence. The tension between the 'Celtic' tradition, and the rigid Church of Scotland—my father's background—and the very distant past of Huguenot, mixed with her Lutheran childhood—my mother's background—brought an interesting mix. The view of my parents at that time, seemed to me, to be that attending church was not necessary, as we were with God all the time.

But this view misses an important biblical principle that tells us to gather together, and function as the Body of Christ, locally as well as globally. My journey has given me a broad view of different denominations, particularly when I include all those that I engaged with in later years.

---

66   1 Corinthians 14:13 tells us to pray that we may interpret what we say. That means it's available!

67   Mark Iles, School for Prophecy, mentioned in Chapter One.

My heavenly Father had a plan. Much of the good in my DNA began to emerge in my heart over those years. The legacy of my great-great-great grandmother and her husband, breaking out of the restrictive mould of Calvinistic religion to start the Evangelical Union Church in Perth in 1856[68], and with her daughter, planting two churches in London, started to emerge in me. I began to fully appreciate the freedom of recognising that we carry our faith even outside the church. I developed a hunger for more of the Spirit, yet I was also able to connect with those in a more restricted environment, and work from within.

Shortly after the HTB conference, I experienced the full eruption of the symptoms of M.E.

A chronic illness, it meant that I was unable to drive, or do simple tasks. By the end, I was not even able to write or climb the stairs. Triggered by viruses of certain kinds, it is a long-term, fluctuating, neurological condition that causes symptoms affecting many body systems, more commonly the nervous and immune systems.[69]

Richard stood by me and helped me, sometimes having to carry me up the narrow stairway. My children were just one and three.

I had been experiencing symptoms for a while before our move to Camberley, but when the power of the Holy Spirit started to move in my life, M.E. developed. This meant we could deal with it.

Healing

It was when I sensed my heavenly Father say, 'This sickness will not end in death,'[70] that I knew He was on the case for my healing. I began to seek it.

---

68   Obituary, 2nd August 1902, *The Late Mrs. Daniel Stewart, Perth*.

69   See Action for M.E., *www.actionforme.org.uk* (last accessed, 11th August 2020).

70   John 11:4

Through our evening fellowship, I was told of a healing ministry that could help. The Holy Spirit was giving me a strong prompt concerning it, and I asked four friends if they wanted to attend a weekend there with me. They said they would drive me there and attend too. We booked, and I began a process they recommended of spending time with God in preparation over the few months before the weekend, asking Him to highlight areas in my life and generations, that He wanted to heal.

Several were highlighted, and I returned from that weekend having experienced a miraculous and lasting healing. So much so that I was capable of the house move that happened three weeks later!

The gift of dance in later years, at the age of forty, was a continuing sign to me and to others, of that healing. Our posting after my healing was to Ripon in North Yorkshire, where we attended Holy Trinity, Ripon, a lively church. I brought my spiritual gifts with me and grew in them with the support of my vicar, David Mann.

This was my history and journey of discovering the Holy Spirit's gifts.

I uncovered one very important factor that was correctly discerned during ministry for healing from M.E., as being in my generational history. Its attachment to me, when cut away by the power of Jesus Christ, released my healing. I was under attack from a particular form of religious spirit. This I will mention here, as it was a crucial piece of the old jigsaw.

This religious spirit was freemasonry. Freemasonry is a religion of works, not connected to the grace gospel that I know and live under.

There had been a darkness, a fogginess, over my life, until it was lifted off by the over-arching power and grace of Jesus Christ. I cannot be silent in my personal testimonies about it. It was essential to remove its effects.[71]

71 My healing was at Ellel Ministries, but there are also excellent resources such as Restoring the Foundations, that can help you tackle generational issues that affect your present. URL: *www.restoringthefoundations.org* (last accessed, 11th August 2020).

I was blessed to have house groups both in Sandhurst and Ripon, who knew and had encountered the seriousness of this issue and understood the dark encounters that result from being under past masonic generations.

Dry Bones

When the gospel of pure grace becomes supplanted with tradition and works, with immovable systems, the life drains out of it, and it becomes simply religion. But when dead bones have the oxygen of grace-life breathed into them, they are raised from the dead.

The religious mindset prevails in the world outside church, and in our lives if we let it. It is a mindset focused on rules and regulations, devoid of fresh life. It is doing things for the sake of doing them, bureaucracy, legalistic thinking, and judgmental attitudes. It can also work itself out (literally!) in our exercise regime and daily habits. We can become very religious about a matter, a task, or an activity, with no real gain. We can perform, without power.

The Holy Spirit is inspirational. Our God brings order out of chaos. He does use structure, yet He is also spontaneous. We cannot live the kingdom life if our personal and organisational lives are rules-bound and legalistic. We need to make the choice to trust the gospel given by the God of grace, in order to break out.

Religion is works-based and has no power. It squeezes out grace. It dislikes the spiritual gifts; they are far too disruptive for its systems-based organisations. The religious mindset will deliberately pinpoint those who are operating in spiritual gifts, to demoralise, disrupt, and at the radical end of the spectrum, destroy them.

The gifts of prophecy and healing, for example, can represent threats to a religious mindset. They cannot sit easily together over the long term. Those who attempt to make changes in such a religious atmosphere will find they face a struggle, even if that is not apparent at the start. That is why good teaching on building kingdom culture is essential. A culture in which the gospel of grace and power can thrive, that will not damage or divide.

The next instalment of my story is given as an example of how bones can have the life-juice of grace squeezed out of them, leaving them dry. It was a long, and serious, lesson from which I have learnt a great deal.

Signs of New Life

The time came to move on from Ripon and we were posted to Tidworth, a big Army garrison. Garrison life can be all-encompassing, and we wanted to find a church outside the army environment, so we looked beyond the boundaries of Tidworth. I was also looking for more stability and wanted to find somewhere in a more central location to where we might be posted in the future—a lot of the Army is based in Wiltshire!

The Anglican village church we settled upon had a reputation of being alive. It was recommended to us by a local lady I had met when she came to speak at our Ladies Fellowship in Camberley. She was now leading a Vineyard house church with her husband not far from us, but at the time, Richard was not quite ready for that as he was of Anglican background.

So, she and her husband helped us get settled. She had received good reports of this Anglican church in a small village up the road, and had visited the vicar to discover what he believed. I am indebted to them for the years which we spent in that church that were fruitful.

The vicar of this Anglican village church had been set alight in his heart by the Spirit, during a visit to Toronto Airport Church at the time of the 'Toronto Blessing', 1994, two years before our arrival. Around that time, I too was being touched by that outpouring at Holy Trinity Brompton. His church administrator and his wife had had the same experience, and they worked closely together. They had opened up the Sunday morning service so people could come to the front and have ministry, and a deluge of people flooded forward to be filled with the Spirit. That was the start of new ways, new experiences, and signs of new life that drew people from the villages around.

By the time we joined there were around one-hundred-and-fifty members, as people like us from the surrounding villages had also joined. We had a worship group with keyboard, guitars, and drums, let alone a clarinet and flute! We sang the latest Michael W. Smith and Vineyard songs. Our vicar's son was a Vineyard church member and a musician. We had a regular monthly midweek church meeting with worship, and some of us were later given the regular opportunity to practice leading the service and teaching in our different styles.

Accustomed to raising my arms in worship, as was common in our previous church, I automatically did the same. I was a singer in the worship group. What I had not realised was that this was not common yet in our new church; people were still in transition. Yet our vicar, being the leader of the group, tended also to be expressive when not playing his guitar, and though this is not a measure of true worship, it started to bring greater freedom and change.

New ground was steadily, gradually broken, until five years later I developed a deeply accepted and supported ten-year dance ministry, where I worked alongside the worship team. It emerged out of a Graham Cooke conference I attended, where I received the gift of dance. My vicar endorsed it, anointing me with oil to minister in the services. By that time, I had also built a relationship with the more traditional eight o'clock congregation. There was a form of comfortable camaraderie and jokes about the possibility of transforming my worship banner poles into fishing rods.

I found people were telling me of their healings, of the gentleness or vibrancy that the dance brought. I would tell them every time that this was a gift and that the energy was a result of the healing I'd received through Jesus from M.E.

A lady recommitted to Christ at her baby son's christening, at which her sister had asked me to dance. Jesus was releasing His real and living power to transform, that goes way beyond religious tradition and stale rote. There was a joy that was beyond me—I was asked to dance at a wedding where the husband began to dance as he left the church with his new wife. It infected and affected, in the power of the Spirit, every time I danced. I knew that this was beyond me, and the life of Jesus was making an impact.

He was in action, and not just through this dance gift, or just me. As some of us would say, 'Aslan is on the move!'[72]

We had a willing leadership, and the golden days seemed as though they would remain; the Spirit blew on the dry bones of religious adherence to tradition. Careful handling was required because we had many old members at the new-style eleven o'clock service, and a much more traditional element that attended the eight o'clock service. I took part in many early-morning communion services, both to prepare my heart and to build bridges with this congregation.

We were all on a roller-coaster in those days—yes, there was opposition, but we were experiencing the power of the Spirit in a small village, and we thought nothing could stop the change. I was given the opportunity to lead, alongside my vicar, what became successful, relational, well-attended daytime courses called 'Saints Alive' in my

72   C.S. Lewis, *The Lion, the Witch and the Wardrobe (Chronicles of Narnia, #1)* (UK: 1950).

home, teaching on life in the Spirit. I cleared out our dining room every week for the children, established a care rota, and then took the rest of the mums to teach them. We grew close. We ran a Holy Spirit day as part of the course, and then I passed the courses along to my co-leader to take them onwards.

I rode the waves happily and ignored the cracks in the foundation,[73] which showed themselves now and then. But you will know, as my readers, where that eventually led. Never ignore the cracks. Seeing them is vital to not falling into them! Experience, wisdom, and most crucially clear and unremitting support from oversight outside the church is vital for carrying a wave of the Spirit in a religious environment. If this is missing, the religious environment can swallow the move and remove the key players.

The Lord of the Dance

One year, one of our very creative and musical priests-in-training developed an 'Unspoken Communion,' which was to be performed outdoors in a garden, for the deanery mission week. He asked me to choreograph dance for it, using the Anglican communion service liturgy and some pieces of wordless music he had chosen.

To say I was excited by the idea would be insufficient. I spent some weeks internalising the liturgy—as a communion server I knew it—practising in our own garden, designing expressive moves to match the powerful words. I then worked with the two leaders showing them the moves that they would perform. It was fun, and significant, and we all really poured ourselves into it. We sensed the power of putting the Word into action.

We performed first in the church chancel, with the congregation,

---

73   Steve Backlund, *Cracks in the Foundation - Reforming Our Thinking to Accelerate Revival* (US: 2014).

our friends, seated in the pews and on chairs and the floor, all around us. As I danced, I was aware of a special atmosphere, which built gradually to the point where, as I passed the cup of wine around the circle, I saw tears formed in people's eyes, slowly falling to the ground, as deep forgiveness for old hurts found outward expression.

Eventually, it was time to perform in the deanery mission week. The garden was more difficult with the ground being uneven for leaps and movements, but the power of the message remained. It was the story of Jesus' death, resurrection, and ascension after all, that I had choreographed by internalising the traditional words of the Anglican communion service.

Our suffragan bishop (responsible for our area) attended, and before he left, he sought me out, as well as the others who had performed with me. Taking me aside a moment, he said, 'Martina, never stop dancing.' He told me how he had received revelation of 'the Lord of the Dance', Jesus, as I leapt from the bonds of death into resurrection life. There were tears behind his eyes.

Soon that bishop was gone. The winds of change blew, and cracks grew wider. Fear, disappointment, and challenge began their work to reveal difficulties that had been there all along.

The bishop was making a clear point to me. He was telling me not only never to stop dancing, but also never to stop exalting Jesus, and bringing the life of the Spirit. He was telling me that that power is what breaks the religious spirit.

Kingdom Culture

New wine must be poured into the right wineskin or the wineskin will crack and leak. I have learnt since those days, through my visits to

Bethel Church, training in kingdom culture online[74] with them, and my years in the School for Prophecy, training and being mentored,[75] that the gifts of the Spirit and the new life that follows His touch thrive in the right culture.

Our village church was the biggest of twelve, all of which were eventually under my vicar's care as team rector and then rural dean, yet only ours developed the new styles of worship as the Spirit moved. Thinking and mindsets were hard to reform, and cracks grew deeper.

The bones had been spoken to, flesh had begun to form on them, and they had been touched by the Spirit's breath—but only partially. The mighty army was wavering because the culture had not transformed with it.

We thought it was changing, we hoped it was, many things happened and healings took place, the prophetic was encouraged (though not always rightly handled), and new systems were in place—but the old systems would just not give up, and we could not seem to heal the wounds.

Tradition versus Common Sense

During our interregnum[76] near the end of our seventeen years in that church, I was leading an early morning Common Book of Prayer service.

I had decided, this time, to prepare a sheet with the full Psalm on it to help the older members who were often still shuffling pages

---

74 See current courses at *www.bethelleadersnetwork.com* (last accessed, August 2020). We spent 2015-2017 on their *Leader Development Courses* with Global Legacy, which is now Bethel Leaders' Network.

75 Mark Iles, prophet, teacher and mentor, founder of the *School for Prophecy*, URL: *www.schoolforprophecy.com* (last accessed, August 2020).

76 The period of time given in the Anglican church between the departure of one vicar and arrival of the next. It is normally a time when a new vicar must be sought, and the committed church members must work together to cover services and the normal operation of the church.

trying to find the place and failing when we were called to speak out the Psalm together. I felt it would help us worship in a more united way, and I placed the sheets at the entrance, one neatly slotted into each Common Book of Prayer.

I could have never imagined the stir it would cause!

Our welcome team member arrived and was the first to have noticed them. 'What's this sheet? We can't have that! They like having exactly the same items every week!'

I told him why we had it and firmly went back to sit in my seat in the chancel, to wait calmly and quietly. I was not prepared to make any changes at this late stage and felt the Spirit encourage me.

The reading of the Psalm went well. I knew these people, and I cared about them. I lived in the village. I'd taken part in the eight o'clock morning service for years now before setting up for the next service, in order to get to know them. I'd sat in the pew with them, and I was a regular communion server.

It may seem a small, almost trivial, example but it was a symptom of a much deeper issue.

What was not understood about the God of our gospel is, He doesn't fit into man-made structure and tradition. Compromise with tradition and you lose the life of the gospel.

Jesus and Religion

The crucial point is, Jesus and religion do not mix.[77] Jesus brought the gospel of grace, with power. Religion brings a gospel of works and tradition, without power. The religious spirit does not like the Holy Spirit. They don't match.

Another time during the interregnum, I was supporting a lady on

77 Read Matthew 23.

our early morning service rota. She had initiated a brief discussion for the first time. That early morning, the congregation consisted of about eight older men and women, so she asked us to sit in the chancel pews before the altar, facing one another. She was an experienced lady who had been a member for much longer than me; I did not expect what came next.

The reading contained Matthew 23:37.

'Jerusalem, Jerusalem, you who kill the prophets and stone those sent to you, how often I have longed to gather your children together, as a hen gathers her chicks under her wings, and you were not willing,' she read, and my heart made a dip wondering how we were going to discuss this verse. The season had been difficult.

The church, by then, had been through a consistory court during our vicar's tenure, over the issue of pew removal. It was a painful episode, but it crystallised the tension between those who wanted to physically and spiritually open things up and those who wanted things to remain the same.

It became very messy. But it clearly demonstrated to me how rules, regulations, and desire to keep things as they have always been can kill off a new move of the Spirit.

The court had taken place beneath the beautiful golden lettering over the arch of the chancel 'To the Glory of God', where I had danced and worshipped for years. The antagonists enlisted the support of a wide range of people. They focused on the heritage of the village, but also gained support from others who held grudges. They won and the pews remained.

It was the time everything changed, it was as if the light that had begun to burn brightly had started to flicker. That day, blood was spilled in the pews where the blood of Jesus' forgiveness and grace should be.

The verse she read out that morning shows both the compassion of Jesus, but also the very clear warning about the consequences of religious behaviour. Not an easy passage to talk about at an early morning traditional service, after a season such as we'd had, but we did.

In a valiant, but mistaken attempt to keep the small congregation of old people at ease, the lady leading ignored those very specific words at the end, 'but you were not willing,' and focused instead on what she felt was the kindness of Jesus wanting to gather them in His arms. She then opened up the discussion. It was silent.

I felt for her. She was being nice. However, unfortunately by this time, the Holy Spirit was prodding me. People were beginning to nod, and I could not let it pass. She asked me to contribute. I carefully but clearly pointed out the final words of the sentence. The same point she had made she made again—that Jesus did not really feel that way.

I knew that I could either remain and be silent, or speak up again. I drew breath, and brought to their attention the context of this passage.

The context is that of Jesus speaking sharply to the pharisees and teachers of the law. The warning was clear in the text. Yes, He was always ready for transformation. Yet if transformation was not at all evident, there were consequences.

He had been rejected. We could not ignore that context. We managed the discussion well, and departed. But it was the beginning of my decision-making process to move out.

The gospel of grace is there, but we have a clear choice to accept it or not. We cannot be 'nice' for the sake of compromise where biblical truth is at stake.

The Truth Sets Free

The gospel of grace does not mean being silent. Jesus really disliked religious behaviour, and He encouraged His disciples to understand this issue. He was outspoken with the religious leaders of His day, just as the Apostle Paul followed in His footsteps in his letter to the Galatians.[78] Paul was clear, publicly, with Peter, about the effects of compromising his faith with religion. We just can't take it lightly.

It is hearing the truth, by God's word, and coming to understand it, that develops faith in our hearts.[79] Jesus says this: 'If you hold to My teaching, you are really My disciples. Then you will know the truth, and the truth will set you free.'[80] This is a Bible verse often taught by my mentor[81] because it contains one condition and two promises. Our part is to hold firmly to His teaching, to live in it. Not only will we then know the truth, we will be set free by the truth. Then, when we speak that truth, it has the power to transform.

We cannot contain the Holy Spirit in a religious box. The new wine needs a new wineskin. When Jesus is misrepresented, we need to stand, and where we stand, we need to do it in love, which is sometimes tough.

If we spend too long in an atmosphere of religion, or indeed any of the traps that I describe in this book, we become blind ourselves. It becomes harder to think clearly and to act with conviction. I know that because I have been a casualty. The truth is, we all make mistakes. Praise God; in the kingdom there is grace, healing, and forgiveness.

My husband and I spent seventeen years there, serving and worshipping. It was a tough decision to make when we moved, and I will share that further journey under the chapter *From Unbelief to Faith*.

We have followed the ups and downs of the church from a distance. But what we know is that with God, there is always hope, there is always grace.

---

78 Galatians 1:6

79 Romans 10:17 NKJV: 'So then faith comes by hearing, and hearing by the word of God'.

80 John 8:31-32

81 Mark Iles, *Developing Your Prophetic Gift* (UK: 2018), chapter on *Battle for Your Mind*, 1.6.1.

I have spoken in this chapter mainly using our church experience as an example because that launched me on a whole new journey and describes the issue and blind spots in the Body of Christ very well. It shows a clear distinction between a religious mindset and the gospel of grace. It shows how dangerous the yeast of a religious mindset can be in church and in life.

The Effect of the Religion Trap

Religion allows no room for grace. Here is the effect of religion on the twelve biblical core life principles, the twelve '*ps*' of my first book in my series. [82]

- Religion restricts the core principle of supernatural *possibilities* in the kingdom of God. It sets up its own diminished and short-sighted kingdom.

- Religion feels that the *purpose* of the church is to follow structure, works, and tradition.

- Religion is afraid of God's *potential* in His created sons and daughters.

- Religion hoards to retain *provision*, there is no trust for supernatural abundance.

- Religion relies on its institution, tradition, and hierarchy for *protection*.

- Religion does not understand God's ways, and cannot flourish in the place of godly *preparation*.

---

82   *The Posture Principle* (UK: 2017), available from *www.zaccmedia.com* or Amazon in the UK, US, and Australia, or direct from me, contact my website at the back of the book.

- Religion promotes the false *promise* of salvation by works. It is another gospel.[83]

- Religion cannot sustain, entertain, nor engage with *prophetic* culture, *prophetic* people, or *prophecies*.

- Religion likes to work by itself, rejecting everything and everyone it does not understand or cannot control. Godly *partnership* is not possible.

- Religion *pursues* itself, not God. It does not obey Jesus' command to seek first the kingdom of God.[84]

- Religion is afraid of the *power* of God. Religion fears its own demise.

- Religion has no *peace*. It cannot partner with the Prince of *Peace*.

The Grace Vertebra

Now for the biblical life principle of grace, and how it affects our perception of the twelve '*ps*':

- Grace recognises *possibility* as hope that is sparkling with expectation, even before it sees the answer.

- Grace understands that everybody is created with a *purpose*, on *purpose*, by a loving God.

- Grace sees the *potential* in a person, even when that person is not demonstrating godly behaviour.

- Grace knows that God's *provision* is not held back just because of what we might have done.

83 Galatians 1:6-7
84 Matthew 6:33

- Grace does not fear that our loving heavenly Father will remove His *protection* on a whim.

- Grace gives space and time for godly *preparation*.

- Grace holds firm to the *promise* of salvation by faith.

- Grace *prophesies* from the heart of the Father, and is the ideal environment for a *prophetic* culture to grow.

- Grace *partners* in the gospel because it understands the Body of Christ.

- Grace *pursues* God hotly. It seeks first the kingdom of God.

- Grace allows the *power* of God to flow without hindrance and is not afraid of it.

- Grace transforms people, places, and situations with its *peace*, resting in the knowledge that God is in control.

Reflect

I'd like you now to take some moments to reflect on your own journey. It may be a long one, or a very short one. What are the twists and turns the path has made? Where have you been aware of His presence and His help? Why have you done certain things? Note those in particular.

How does your church come around you? Do they support you? Why or why not? Consider how you are building bridges in your community and church. How are your relationships? Allow these things to pass through your mind.

Read the Grace Vertebra and Religion Trap statements again. Let the Holy Spirit speak within you.

Activate

Over the coming month, read and meditate on the Apostle Paul's letter to the Galatians. Read it in several different translations, including The Message version, and The Passion Translation. Both are online on the Bible App.[85]

At the start of this exercise, spend some time with God and ask the Holy Spirit to guide you throughout that month. Then, use a journal to record anything you hear. Ask Him for practical insight and wisdom in your own journey. Allow Him to change and transform your heart. Give Him time. Let your heavenly Father enfold you in His big arms. Just sit with Him. Take times of silence, when all you do is receive His love. Like pressing the download button on a laptop, wait for Him to drop in His messages of delight.

QUESTION

» How did you encounter the Holy Spirit?

» What has been your experience in or out of the church and how has it affected your journey?

» How have you spoken up when the Holy Spirit has prompted you to take action?

» How have you resisted speaking up, when it has not been the Holy Spirit leading, and waited for the right moment?

85 The Bible App (last accessed, 8th August 2020).

FROM UNBELIEF TO FAITH

'And now abide faith, hope, love, these three;...'

1 Corinthians 13:13 NKJV

CHAPTER FIVE

THE FAITH VERTEBRA

'Commit your way to the Lord; trust in Him
and He will do this...'
PSALM 37:5

Healing and Salvation Out of Loss

The journey from unbelief to faith is our greatest.

To highlight its importance, I will share a painful story as my testimony. I cannot write a book on identity, and not mention the enormity of this event in our lives. But out of it, has come healing and salvation not only for us, but for others with whom we have been connected. That is the life lesson for this chapter, and I will share with you some of the resulting testimonies.

It was while experiencing the numbing pain of observing the features of my eight-week-old son Robert, in the 'waiting' room before he was moved to the hospital morgue that my faith was sorely tested.

Running down the underground corridors from the accommodation to the Paediatric Intensive Care Unit in the dead of night in response to an urgent phone call had been a common event. I had lived in the old Brompton Hospital in London for around four weeks, and in Maidstone hospital for the previous two when our son was admitted at two weeks old. Now, there seemed to be nothing.

You see, I had spent hours in the chapel at the Brompton Hospital telling God that I believed He would heal him. By sheer willpower and the dislike of imagining what it would be like to lose him, I had clung on! Operation after operation on Robert's back-to-front heart had left him weak until a serious infection swept through the intensive care unit and killed six babies. Robert was the fifth, after giving part of his lung for tests in a vain effort to save the sixth.

It was Nicky Lee, from Holy Trinity Brompton, who prayed with me for him before he went into his last operation. You, as my readers, again know the story. I did not know his church then. Four years later, I was back at Brompton, through an invitation completely out of the blue, but across the road in Holy Trinity Church.

How do God-incidences like that happen? How was it, that the life of our first son that we lost in Brompton came to be restored in double measure with our two—now adult—sons, and that my encounters with the power of the Holy Spirit that changed my life, happened across the road in the same place, in Holy Trinity Church, Brompton?

Our Father knows exactly what will help each one of us understand His deep compassion and passion for us. He was showing me, 'Martina! I SAW you. I SEE you. I KNOW.' I knew He too had lost his only Son. I knew deep inside that He understood. Though my faith was tested and to an extent numbed at the time of loss, it never died.

It returned stronger, and more effective, to steal back from the darkness that which is God's. In the writing and editing of this book, my husband has challenged and chewed concepts with me, and one question was this: why did I not lose my faith? I cannot make light of this for the sake of readers who may have themselves experienced this magnitude of loss.

My heart response is this: because I'd had experience of Him. I knew Him in a relationship, where, though I was not perfect, He always kept His promise to me. Even when I felt the bottom fall out of everything, in the most painful times, He'd shown me that He was there in it with me. He had taught me already, that I couldn't, wouldn't, ever know 'why' things happen. But I could be assured that He had them in hand and would bring the best out of them.

When Robert's death happened, I received it with a depth of anguish that was physical and long. Yet a process began even through the alternating pain and numbness that would not let go. It was inbred in me from my first memorable encounter with Jesus at the age of five, and probably even before. It had showed itself in that Brompton hospital chapel in the way I prayed for Robert. For I knew that to let go, to let ourselves be swept away with trauma is the end.

This was one of God's signatures on my soul that has stood the test of time: His faithfulness to bring redemption out of what the enemy meant to harm me. I may have limited understanding, and will one day know in full, but as for me, I trust Him.

He knew when I was born that this would happen. He went ahead and prepared me. He planted a tiny golden seed of faith in me at the time of that very first memory of an encounter with Jesus at five years old. He spoke to me through a colouring I was making, and the words I wrote, 'Jesus is my Friend. He has put His name upon me. Jesus is King of all kings!' It says everything. I have a relationship with the most powerful King in the universe, and I held on to that. There was simply a flicker that just never died.

We have an enemy, as Jesus called him, who comes to kill, steal, and destroy. Yet, God, our King, trumps him by promising us abundant life.[86] The death of my firstborn son did not prove that God does not exist. Many could question, why not? But in my heart I already had experience that He did exist. I just needed time to grapple with the consequences of loss.

I cried, I allowed the full impact of grief. I wrote all about it in my journal, letting out every detail while we spent the following two weeks in a remote part of France. I returned, and took up temping, where I could get on with a job and focus without the need to settle. I began a distance-learning writing course and spent hours typing. I wrote a feature article about our experience for the Kent Messenger, where I'd become a freelance contributor, so that my wonderful old people I'd come to know at my early morning swims during my pregnancy could understand. I wrote about my faith that God and the doctors had not let me down. We faced the Daily Mail on our doorstep, and we told them too, when they came to interview us.

Eventually, I left my temping job and became a full-time freelance writer. I began my journey back into church, and moved house again! Just over a year after the loss of Robert, James was born, vibrantly healthy, then two years later, David bounced into life!

Brompton was a place of deep loss, and then four years later, of the start of a new understanding of the power of God through His Holy Spirit and of my choice, to walk in it. That is not coincidence. One thing I did do was to open myself up for healing, not only physically in 1994 from M.E., but also emotionally and spiritually shortly afterwards. I followed up with a healing retreat where we spent a week focusing in on spiritual and emotional areas, as well as breaking off generational effects, curses, and faulty beliefs.

The journey of grief was not easy and it left its scar. Yet I recognise a good Father, and I recognise an enemy—as Jesus calls him—who

86   John 10:10

kills, steals, and destroys. My Father God restores over and above, neutralising and overpowering the effects of tragedy. Our scars are offered for the healing and comfort of others.[87]

Stories of Healings and Transformation

'Martina! My back is healed this morning!' cried the voice on the end of the line. Once again, Jesus had acted in response to a simple hand laid on and a command of healing in the middle of a carpark in Ripon.

My fellow ladies' group member, from Holy Trinity Ripon and I were returning from the local nursery school where we had picked up our children. She was pregnant and suffering badly with her back. Now she was overjoyed at having a pain-free back!

In my time in Ripon[88], I began to consider what I was seeing and the immediate and miraculous healing I had personally received just before moving there—the healing that had not only overcome the disempowerment and disability of M.E., but had increased the gift of healing and the prophetic as a by-product!

I decided to pursue my calling as a writer. So, I sought out an excellent childminder for my youngest son, David, to give me two hours a week in which to write.

I walked in with David on his first morning, having had an initial meeting and a short conversation the previous week.

She stunned me when she said, 'I gave my life to Christ after we had our meeting, Martina. I've got so many questions for you.'

I tried hard not to fall over backwards. All I had done in our brief conversation was say why I would like her to look after David for that short time. That I was a Christian, a believer in Jesus Christ, and that

---

87 If you are struggling with the loss of a baby, please do connect with me at *www.gracecreativity.com*.

88 See chapter *From Religion to Grace*, for this story and the conference at Holy Trinity Brompton.

I wanted to tell people about Him and give my testimonies. I also told her that I had been healed in Jesus' name and that I couldn't keep quiet.

She proved to become a powerful and effective agent in God's kingdom, joining Holy Trinity Church, Ripon and going on to write her own books. She is described by her publisher as being passionate for evangelism and she co-founded Church on the Net in 2007.

That is how Jesus works. It is simple. Just speak, just act. It is His work; we are the ones who activate it through faith, and become His agents. We may just touch one person. But that person may touch many more than we ever will. Keep it simple.

We were members of the lively church, Holy Trinity Ripon. I often spoke to our vicar, David Mann, about the Holy Spirit, and he stood by me in my growth in using the gifts. I enjoyed being involved in a large daytime ladies' group and hosted one of the house groups in our home. We were active in the gifts and experienced healings.

One day, David and I had a meeting. He was grinning widely and gave me a hug, 'Martina, just make sure next time you've got me with you!' he said, as I came to him looking sheepish. A lady had gone to him, because when she'd asked for prayer concerning her fear, and I prayed with her in the name of Jesus, she had seen a white cross, fallen over, and been delivered! Unfortunately, she appeared to be more afraid of Jesus when he actually became active in her life than of her fear.

David was extremely supportive, and a great friend of our very young boys, whom he would pick up and swing around at the end of the service, just as a dad would. He held packed prayer meetings in the crypt every week, where the gifts were used. God was moving in this church, and he did not feel the need to use ungodly control. We had uncertain people, as well as strong Spirit-filled, mature people, journeying side by side in this Anglican church.

These stories find their way in here because they were the direct result of a mustard seed of faith, a choice in 1994 to walk in the power of the Holy Spirit, not just in word. At my healing, I had heard from my Father God that I would need to stand on the truth of what was done as it would be contested. Over the initial months, it was indeed contested with the enemy's lies at opportune times, and I learnt to stand firm in my healing and carry that over into faith for the healing of others. You can too.

Climbing Out from Under the Table

While in Ripon, I visited a place every Friday evening called Hollybush Farm, where they had a visiting speaker each week. I was very hungry and learning fast.

One of those speakers was John Glass, a Pentecostal minister and Superintendent of the Elim Pentecostal Churches, Scotland, and he prayed with me. He was given a picture by the Holy Spirit of me emerging from under a table, out of an egg, to become who I was always meant to be. He heard that I was being released from the 'snare of the fowler'. This he took time to explain to me. The snare, was the fear of man—pleasing people and fear of what they think—that stopped me from flying. The picture explained that I would become an example as I was released, so that others would learn to be who they were created to be.

He had written about this snare in his books.[89] The 'snare' is basically faith in the wrong place. Being afraid of what people think is putting their opinion above faith in God. This can be expressed in, or eventually emerges as, unbelief. The journey into the freedom that John Glass spoke about in his prophecy has taken longer than I expected, revealing a specific category of unbelief that needed a complete, foundational, digging-up.

89   John Glass, *Saying Yes, Saying No* (UK: 1990), and *Open Hands, Open Heart* (UK: 1988).

The Roundabout of Unbelief

The process truly began at our village church that I have mentioned in the previous chapters when we were mid-way through a 'Freedom in Christ' course. I remember it as another period of hope, where we believed we might solve our problems as a church; divisions and discomfort amongst the team of churches had been prolonged.

I was already very familiar with the concepts taught on the course, having been using Neil Anderson's book 'Living Free in Christ' regularly whilst backing our church counsellor both as a prophetic intercessor, and for her work at a healing centre nearby. It was encouraging that we were all in it together.

However, it was during that course, that I began to understand how the culture we are part of affects how God's Word is received.

As I drove round the roundabout that leads into our village, I heard the words in my spirit, 'roundabout of unbelief'. I saw an image of people going round and round in circles, never having the faith to fully stand upon what they have as an inheritance in Christ. I told no one.

I held the words over the years, wondering why this was something I needed to know. I thought it was me, and I sought God and acted in the faith that I knew.

Years later, I have learnt that a culture, an environment, needs to be conducive to the gifts of the Spirit. That way, the gifts and people can flourish best. Remaining within a culture that is tainted with the yeast of political and religious spirits over the long term means that we will also be contaminated. The biblical result of this is spiritual blindness, and we are taken on the roundabout of unbelief.

The truth of our standing and identity in Christ was not fully comprehended, stood on, nor activated, even after the Freedom in Christ course, which meant that operating in the Spirit did not have a secure basis—particularly as it became clear in the years following, that we did not have the full and committed, continuous, support from our regional oversight.

We need to know where to find shelter from prevailing winds, or we get bent out of shape. We need courage to move to that shelter.

I used to find, in certain situations, making decisions difficult. In that church, because of the prevailing winds, I did find them particularly hard. I could make good decisions, but once I had done so, another process kicked in. Was I sure that this suited everyone? What if—?

Fear made these doubts seem huge because fear is the enemy's prime weapon. When he has a hold somewhere, then he has a launching pad for his arrows.

If we have allowed our identity in Christ to be eroded or we don't understand the enormity of the sacrifice of Jesus and the inheritance we carry as sons and daughters of God, then we won't be using our God-given shield of faith to quench those flaming arrows to the best of our ability.[90]

Though it is often hard to accept where we have been, I believe we must find the courage to face and deal with our past, our hindrances, our hang-ups; then we will be richly rewarded. If we are able to move on to use the lessons we have learnt, to serve one another, the kingdom grows. We can always learn from our mistakes. Only religion fears getting it wrong.

One of my favourite quotes, on this topic, is from Brené Brown:

> '*Owning our story can be hard but not nearly as difficult as spending our lives running from it. Embracing our vulnerabilities is risky but not nearly as dangerous as giving up on love and belonging and joy—the experiences that make us the most vulnerable. Only when we are brave*

90 Ephesians 6:16

enough to explore the darkness will we discover the infinite power of our light.'[91]

Loyalty

I began to sense internal unrest. Our church went through difficult times and I remained, wanting to see it through. I was often on my face in the chancel in those days, along with others. However, there came a time when I found myself flat on my face on the grass at the top of the ridge where I used to run in the early morning. I was heavy-hearted, and the run was not helping this time.

'There MUST be more than this!' I shouted all my frustration into the wind. Inter-warring within the team and the consistory court over the pews were not what I had given my life to Jesus for. The political and religious spirits were alive and active, and my health was suffering along with my faith.

I'd lost sight of how life in the Spirit had once been, before I arrived there, and was blind to the constriction that had been closing around me. A slow and deathly squeeze.

On the face of it, these things were shifty and unclear, difficult to pinpoint and often, particularly because of loyalty and friendships, hard to quantify or act upon. That is usually the way in these circumstances.

Over the next year, I found Father was calling our family to new pastures; that we needed a rest and reset. Confirmations were coming from people we knew outside the village and our church, all who cared about us. Two of those had known me for over twenty years. Yet I could not find the courage to make the move; it felt disloyal. The years of being under the influence had removed the courage for change that we once exuded.

91   Brené Brown, *The Gifts of Imperfection* (2018).

I was actually in a state of unbelief. Father had spoken, He saw, and He knew what was happening to us. Finally, I made my first move. I stepped back from all my duties for a year, during which I took a long, hard, look into the Bible and there began my journey of restoration and healing.

The State of Unbelief

The book of Proverbs always offers an opposite to whatever problem it describes in each verse. The opposite to the fear of man as a snare, is to trust in the Lord as safety.[92] In another verse, the fear of the Lord (awe) is described as, 'a fountain of life, turning a person from the snares of death.'[93] The focus of our lives must be on seeking the kingdom first (fountain of life). Not approval of people (snare of death). This should resolve any decisions we ever need to take!

There is an obvious Scripture to highlight in this chapter on the trap of unbelief. It is in the letter of James.[94]

James points out that when we need wisdom, i.e. to make a choice as to how to act, we must believe when we ask, and not doubt. He repeats the issue twice for emphasis! He then describes what we are like, when in doubt. We are like a wave of the sea, tossed to and fro, blown by the wind!

Then he issues the crunch point—which is actually simply the consequence, or our choice, not the meanness of our Father—that we shouldn't expect to receive anything from the Lord if we don't have belief.

My experience is that the Father doesn't remove Himself from us,

92 Proverbs 29:25
93 Proverbs 14:27
94 James 1:5-7

but that we simply cannot receive from Him because receiving from Him requires faith in what He speaks.[95]

This is down to us, our responsibility, and like the father did for his son in the Bible story, we must cry out, 'Jesus! Help me to believe![96] Let Your Holy Spirit believe within me and groan for me![97]'

In a state of paralysing unbelief and indecision, we are naturally double-minded and unstable in all we do.

We do not live in condemnation, because there IS no condemnation in Christ Jesus.[98] So get to it, and take a small, wobbly step and see where it takes you. That's what I had to do.

New Pastures

During that year out, I enjoyed the freedom to seek and be still, and to busy myself with the every-day jobs of caring for my family and home. I loved the times I spent in God's presence. The confusion that had built up within me, and the effects of restriction and condemnation, rose to the surface. During this time, I was alone, or with family and very close, long-term, friends, or within the Ffald-y-Brenin community in Pembrokeshire. Jesus felt very near.

After seven months, I booked myself on a Ffald-y-Brenin conference where I sought God for my future, followed by a prophetic conference at Bath City Church. It was 2012, and Liz Evans had invited two prophets to speak, minister, and teach, Mark Iles and Carl Wills.

It was the evening meeting in the auditorium of that conference that the Holy Spirit intervened.

Sitting quietly off to the side, tired after the day, I spotted Mark

95 Matthew 9:28
96 See the story in Mark 9:14-29.
97 Romans 8:26
98 Romans 8:1

walking past. All he did was lay his hand on my shoulder briefly, and say, 'That's a great place to get some quiet'.

The effect was enormous. A Holy Spirit flicker of a spark caught, and a spiritual fire was re-ignited. I knew something had happened, but I didn't know the journey I was about to take.

Next day, Liz suggested that those who were interested in mentoring should ask Mark for details. My feet took me over to him to ask for those details. That spark had caught the touch-paper of a Martina I no longer remembered, and the flame grew.

It was another year before Mark became my mentor. By that time, after a roundabout of decision-making, our new vicar had given us her blessing to move from the village church we had served for seventeen years and on to new pastures.

Richard and I joined Bath City Church in 2013, where we were given the opportunity to bask in the Spirit-filled atmosphere for eighteen months, receiving the healing that we so needed.

We then started our journey settling into and becoming members of the Vineyard Church.

My mentoring journey came to an end in 2020 after seven years. In that time, I have dug out my faulty foundations, settled more deeply into my identity in Christ, and now carry the authority as a child of my heavenly Father in greater measure. I have trained in the prophetic ministry, and am being launched into training as a prophetic teacher with others on the School for Prophecy team.

My husband and I run our business. I am a visual artist, a writer. We serve our church in a different manner to the way we used to serve. We are both on the prophetic team and the connect team. That is all! And that is enough. For now.

Faith Comes by Hearing, and Hearing by the Word of God

We think we hear many things. Yet oftentimes they do not register. Actually *hearing* speaks of really letting what we have heard sink down inside, and find a lodging place, out of which action emerges. Really hearing produces understanding and wisdom, and faith.

The best way to strengthen our 'hearing', is by meditating on God's Word. Both on the written Scriptures, but also on those things He has spoken personally to us in the form of promises and tested prophecies.

Revelation is that which ignites what we hear, to become a living spiritual organism. It drives our faith, through conviction, to action.

The way out of unbelief is one of holding fast to the truth and not allowing outside influences to push it aside. Of keeping our eyes fastened on the kingdom first, at all times. Whatever the consequence.

The Block

Unbelief is not only described as a sin, which actually simply means 'missing the mark', but it also blocks the flow to hearing, to understanding, to revelation, to faith, to conviction, to action. It diverts our energies into anxiety, fear, worry—all the same root—that allow the waters of energy that flow from revelation to drain into dry and unproductive earth.

We spend hours pleading with God for wisdom in our decisions, when He has already spoken. We stay awake at night thinking we are not hearing, because we are perhaps afraid to take that step!

What prevents us? What fear stops us from believing? There are many, according to our background and history. I have described in this book those traps that have prevented me from moving into what I now know to be true.

The biggest obstacle I know, that runs through them all, is a taskmaster who is never lenient: fear of man.

Jesus asks us to believe Him. To have faith. Faith is what we live by.[99]

Though our faith may be as small as a mustard seed right now, particularly in the season in which I write this, that of the COVID-19 pandemic, our heavenly Father has a strategy in place. He has anointed people to come to our rescue, unlock the door of the trap, take us by the hand, lead us into the understanding and authority of our identity in Him, and release us to fly. But for the strategy to be enacted, we need faith.

The Effect of the Unbelief Trap

Unbelief pulls everything out of shape. Before showing you the beauty of the faith vertebra, I will point out the effects of unbelief on the twelve principles, the twelve '*ps*' of my first book in the series, *The Posture Principle*.

- Unbelief doubts the whisper of *possibility* and keeps us in the trap of 'impossible'.

- Unbelief denies that God will fulfil our *purpose*.

- Unbelief never hears the words that God speaks over us and through others to us, about our *potential*.

- Unbelief is a spirit of lack, not heaven-sent *provision*.

- Unbelief tells us that we are bereft and helpless, without *protection*.

- Unbelief thinks that *preparation* means we always need to be alert to bad surprises.

99 Romans 1:17, 5:2; Galatians 3:11, amongst others.

- Unbelief speaks of an unfaithful, uncommitted, Covenant-breaker God who never keeps His *promise*.

- Unbelief steals faith in *prophecy*.

- Unbelief partners with comparison and jealousy through low self-worth, and so *partnership* with others becomes a threat.

- Unbelief has no energy to *pursue* because it is so wound up in itself going around in circles and getting sick on the seas of despondency.

- Unbelief is a diminishing spirit with no *power*, and no capability.

- Unbelief cannot find *peace*. It is always searching round the next corner looking for the answer and never finding it.

The Faith Vertebra

Our fifth lumbar vertebra sits atop our pelvis and provides the base. This faith vertebra sits perfectly at the point of our spiritual spine that connects with walking; the faith walk.

So let's talk about how faith affects the twelve principles in my first book,[100] the twelve '*ps*', and then we will have some reflection time:

- Faith means, everything is *possible* in God, according to His purposes.

- Faith says, God has a *purpose* for us, that He is committed to bring to pass.

- Faith tells us we have enormous, untapped *potential* that our Father in heaven is drawing out.

100 Martina Davis, *The Posture Principle* (UK: 2017).

- Faith speaks *provision* over us, where our Triune God, who lives within us, will provide everything we need.

- Faith lets us know, all is well, we are in our Father's hands, and we have the King of kings to *protect* us.

- Faith commits to *preparation*. It takes preparation to come into purpose, and our full potential.

- Faith holds our hand with *promise*. He is a faithful God.

- Faith releases us into greater vision through the words that God speaks over us in *prophecy*.

- Faith restores relationship and opens up *partnerships* with others for mutual support and ministry.

- Faith *pursues* God with one focus.

- Faith impacts the world with *power* through the Holy Spirit, breaking open and releasing others into freedom, healing, and fullness of life.

- Faith opens the way for the Prince of *Peace* to rule in our hearts and minds.

Reflect

Faith is core to everything. This spiritual vertebra, coming as it does in the last chapter, helps our imagery in this reflection time. In our physical body, that final vertebra of our lumbar spine is the largest. Being at the base, just above where we sit, we can imagine ourselves 'seated' in faith.

So reflect now on that. We are seated in the heavenly places in Christ Jesus. We sit deep into the rest of the Lord

Jesus, where we learn from Him. Only out of that place, and that place alone, can we live authentically and freely. Take time to imagine that.

Faith can only come by hearing, and hearing by the Word of God, with the Holy Spirit bringing revelation. When we start to do the work of renewing our minds with biblical truth, we access the Identity Key already placed inside of us.

Reflect on your own journey, and where you have found faith rise up in you. Hold onto those times.

Activate

Take some time to look at each of the twelve principles above, both how they are affected negatively by unbelief and how they flourish through faith.

Take time to search the Bible for what God has to say on these. Read verses out loud over the course of the weeks during which you are working with this chapter. Allow them to settle down into your mind and heart. Hear what the Spirit is saying to you. Write in your journal about them.

Start to practice daily stillness times. These are times when you go deep down into your inner self, where God is. They are times when you may not be aware of anything spoken, simply aware of His presence. Instead of music, you can repeat a word or phrase in order to take you into His presence, after which relax in that place of presence, until you need to use the phrase again.

Do not be anxious about thoughts that come into your mind. I remember one of the desert fathers saying that these thoughts are like flies, simply bat them away mentally with the word or phrase you are repeating. Stay focused on God's presence. This is for a purpose, though it can seem impossible to understand. God is full of mystery.

It is up to you how long you take over silence in God's presence. I suggest you start with just ten minutes.

As the writer of Psalms tells us[101]:

> *'Trust in the Lord and do good; dwell in the land and enjoy safe pasture. Take delight in the Lord, and He will give you the desires of your heart.'*

There is deep peace in that.

He continues,

> *'Commit your way to the Lord; trust in Him and He will do this... Be still before the Lord and wait patiently for Him...'*[102]

QUESTION

» Have you found yourself in the trap of unbelief in any way?

» Are you willing to take a step out? And take another, and another, into faith?

» When can you find time to put God first and arrange to spend silent time with Him?

---

101 Psalm 37:3-4
102 Psalm 37:5,7a

CONCLUSION

Our identity in Christ is the core of this book. It is the key. The key that unlocks the prison gates of the five traps I have described.

Serving as a son or daughter of our heavenly Father in Jesus Christ, filled with the Holy Spirit, is what makes us the unexpected warriors I described at the start of this series. We are those who do not win by strength, fame, or qualification. We win because Jesus won for us, and we have been set free to become the real children of God we were created to be. We do this by the power of the Holy Spirit, using His weapons, which are not of this world. We have His resurrection power.

This is why we must take care to avoid the five traps. Through the experience of my own journey, I have come to understand that without knowing, hearing, and understanding who Jesus Christ is, who our heavenly Father is, and who the Holy Spirit is, we will not be able to claim our true identity.

I structured *The Posture Principle* around the twelve core principles that reveal who God really is for us, and the depth of His goodness. A meditative guidebook, it is designed to inspire a mindset-change from how we often think about God, according to our experiences, history, and the lies we have taken on board, to one of knowing our truest calling: intimacy with God.

Those who try to understand spiritual things with their minds will find a closed door. To truly understand, you must open the door to the Holy Spirit, then you will see freshly. Ask Him to show you. He always responds.

This book goes one step further. In it, we confront the traps that keep us from our full identity in Christ, and we tackle the challenges that prevent us from seeing clearly. I have illustrated it throughout with stories and testimonies from my life. I hope this has made it more relatable.

At its heart, it is about mindsets, habits, and how we begin to climb out of the boxes around our lives.

In order to truly walk free of the fear of man, out of the mindsets of performance, punishment, duty, religion, and unbelief, it is essential to have the backbone, the knowledge of who we are in Christ, and that He will never leave us.

He supports us with all He has and is. He is a loving Father who always protects. He is excited about His children, and loves it when we throw our all upon Him and come to Him first and foremost.

If we do not know who we are called in Christ, what our purpose is as a child of God, what Jesus has truly done for us on the cross, or understand our authority in Him and our eternal future, then we cannot see clearly, and move into freedom.

As my mentor has said to me many times, 'Freedom is the end game.' My third and final book in this, the *Equipping Unexpected Warriors* series, will cover this area more fully! Prepare to walk in 'Freedom'!

Martina Davis,
August 2020

ABOUT THE AUTHOR

Martina Davis is a Christian author, artist, and photographer with a heart for prophetic ministry. She reconnects people with the presence of God, equipping them with tools to release their identity as His sons and daughters, bring freedom, and expose unhealthy mindsets. She has been married to Richard for thirty-five years and together they have had three sons. Her faith journey and wide church experience gave her the inspiration to start Grace Creativity, through which she exercises her ministry and business. She also serves the wider Church as part of the School for Prophecy, UK, both in prophetic ministry and as a teacher. Martina and Richard serve their home church, Winchester Vineyard, on the prophetic team.

Contact Martina at:
www.gracecreativity.com

ALSO BY MARTINA DAVIS

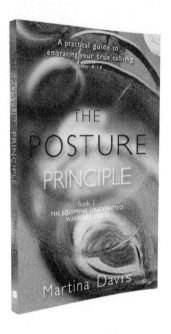

THE POSTURE PRINCIPLE
A Practical Guide to Embracing Your True Calling
By Martina Davis

Many of us are hidden under false identity, have a skewed view of God, and do not understand how to reach out and take our inheritance and speak freedom to others. Out of my own journey and experience, I seek to equip so that we all may grow up in Christ together, and be ignited to bring light into darkness. 'Equipping Unexpected Warriors' is a series of three books about our Posture, Identity and Freedom, as called and chosen children of a living God.

ISBN 978-1-911211-71-6 / 148pp paperback

Printed in Great Britain
by Amazon